ONCE UPON A TIME,

THE PATENT

PASCAL ATTALI

ISBN : 979-8-831-97177-4

To my parents,
who gave me the taste for writing.

To my wife and children,
who allow me to satisfy it.

« Il faut faire aujourd'hui ce que tout le monde fera demain »
("Do today what everyone else will do tomorrow")

Jean Cocteau

FOREWORD

In this well-documented book, Pascal Attali invites us to learn about the history of the patent, which – over time – has helped to make technology a catalyst for social and economic progress. The author provides a pedagogical account of the successive developments and key milestones that led to the creation of the patent as we know it today, without neglecting the fundamental role played by France.

A key industrial property right, the patent has evolved considerably – from the system of monopolies granted by cities in antiquity, through to privileges in the Middle Ages and then royal charges and letters patent during the Ancien Régime, right up until the first French law instituting a "patent of invention" at the end of the 18th century. For the first time, a patent was then considered a property right and no longer the mere granting of a privilege. This protection of inventors and their inventions paved the way for the emergence of an industrial property system that would provide a crucial legal basis for the Industrial Revolution and play an important role in society. Because patents make it possible to foster innovation, capitalize on inventions and share scientific and technological advances, while also respecting creators' rights – all for the common good.

As we advance through the book's pages, the author goes beyond the historical aspects to help us gain a better understanding of patents in the 21st century. In addition to presenting the various stakeholders and explaining the role of the state, he invites the reader to reflect on the protection of innovation and the alternatives to patenting. He also provides an overview of the new uses for patents – how they can serve a company's business strategy, become a monetization tool or help speed up cooperation. Lastly, he explains how the patent has adapted to the technological revolutions of the modern era and touches on the associated technological, geopolitical, environmental, health and inflation issues.

I thank Pascal Attali for giving everyone access to the story of the patent's creation and transformation. His book serves a valuable purpose. Understanding the past makes it easier to see what's ahead, so that we can more effectively address the challenges we face both today and in the future. I recognize in this work the talent for teaching and the desire to share knowledge that make Pascal one of the standout trainers at our INPI Academy.

This book is perfectly aligned with INPI's goal of raising awareness about the protection and promotion of innovation. It was therefore only natural for us to be associated with its publication.

Enjoy your read!

Pascal Faure
CEO of the French Patent and Trademark Office (INPI)

INTRODUCTION

The job you have is part of the image you project to the people around you, including your own family. At the beginning of my professional life, my title of "junior telecommunications engineer" earned me a certain esteem from my relatives (as well as many requests to repair their new cell phones). So it came to them as a shock when, only a few years after starting a promising career in the telecoms industry, I announced that I wanted to change path and work in the field of patents. It is true that, in the early 2000s, intellectual property and patents in particular were still poorly understood by the general public in France; to a certain extent, this is still the case, unlike in the United States where you only have to tell the first person who comes along that you are a "patent attorney" for them to immediately start explaining how they made or could have made a fortune using patents. Still, my choice caused a great deal of perplexity and confusion. For example, my manager told me that he did not understand why I was going to waste my talents in the dull position of a "paper-pusher".

As far as I am concerned, I have never regretted my transition, which made me discover an exciting world at the crossroads of the technical, legal and economic fields. I have also encountered fascinating people, starting with those who gave me my chance at a new career by recruiting me, and to whom I am deeply grateful.

However, the change did not happen without its problems. Coming from the very young and dynamic telecoms sector, I was first struck by the fact that in the IP firm I joined, there were professionals of all ages with sharp minds. My colleagues were as comfortable interpreting law as they were understanding complex technical standards. They were capable of drafting expert texts in several languages, discussing technical details with an engineer and presenting a sophisticated strategy to a CEO. This mix of styles, especially the ability of my new colleagues to launch themselves into futuristic technologies while remaining part of an old tradition (some of them were still using tape recorders to draft their patents!), seemed strange at first. Nonetheless, it soon gave me a bizarre sense of belonging to and participating in an enterprise that went far beyond the scope of my personal work, a kind of collective construction that had its roots in the past and built bridges to the future.

About a year after I started at the firm, during a family gathering, young cousins of mine, some of them still children, asked me about my curious career path. What exactly was my new job? The question seems simple. My answer was awkward. To put the matter to rest, I answered briefly that I helped inventors protect their inventions. "Why do they need your help, aren't they the inventors?" they asked. "Yes, of course they are the inventors, but I help them shape their ideas and turn them into products you can buy", I replied. A long silence followed. I mentally looked for a more convincing explanation that they could understand. My thinking was interrupted by the youngest: "That sounds cool! So, what's your most famous invention?", he said with an enthusiasm that caught me off guard. I hesitated to correct again: I was not the inventor and could not claim credit for any invention, let alone a famous one. Moreover, the inventions I had helped patent so far related to small improvements, mostly dealing with complex, abstract telecoms processes that were often invisible for the end user. In short, I had nothing that could satisfy the legitimate curiosity of my interlocutors. It was a lost cause. I was assessing the situation at full speed and, out of ideas, I finally opted for an easy solution. I said that I had contributed to the invention of the cell phone!

This way out was not an outright lie, since the first work I was assigned did indeed concern inventions related to mobile telephony. In any case, it got me out of the dead end in which I had unwittingly put myself. More surprisingly, it earned me a whole new esteem among my cousins, who were suddenly proud to have such a creative elder in their family. As one might expect, this glory did not stand the test of time. It quickly faded away, and finally disappeared, probably when my cousins' education gave them enough critical thinking to question my claim, or maybe when, a few years later, the launch of the smartphone made the first cell phones (my "invention"!) completely obsolete.

In retrospect, the embarrassment I felt while trying to explain my activity to a young audience was likely due to two difficulties: the first concerning the nature of invention and the second concerning the concept of patent.

As far as the nature of invention is concerned, it is not so easy to understand. Of course, inventions seem familiar to us, being present in our daily lives, whether in the press or in the many manufactured products we use. Inventions have always arisen out of all times and places. As a technical expression of creativity, inventiveness is perhaps what best characterizes humanity. Certainly, some animals show an astonishing ingenuity, like monkeys able to make tools to break nuts. But humankind's ability to systematically look for solutions to the problems we identify does not seem to have an equivalent in other species. As historian Yuval

Noah Harari explains in his famous book "*Sapiens: A Brief History of Humankind*", this human peculiarity may date back to the cognitive revolution, an evolutionary leap in the way our brains work that occurred about 70,000 years ago. While the stone tools carved by our ancestors were more or less the same for nearly 2 million years, from the cognitive revolution onwards, inventions followed one another at an ever increasing pace, enabling us first to make the tools necessary for our survival, then to build boats that could cross the oceans and spread all over the Earth, and finally to conceive spaceships that yesterday took us to the Moon and tomorrow will certainly take us to Mars!

And yet, our relationship to inventions is not univocal. While today they are associated with the positive notions of technical progress and economic development, inventions have long had more negative connotations, associated with cunning and lies. It is true that they express both sublime elements of human genius and sometimes more petty goals. For instance, while the race for vaccination against the 19th century plagues of rabies, cholera and tuberculosis, which was led in parallel by the French scientist Louis Pasteur and the German physician Robert Koch, was motivated by a genuine desire to save lives, it was not without rivalry that went beyond mere mutual stimulation.

How then can invention be defined? It differs from the abstract idea, which it aims to embody in a particular form. But it does not go so far as to designate the actual implementation or commercialization of this form, which belongs to the realm of "innovation", according to the somewhat artificial distinction made by the economist Joseph Schumpeter. Invention is therefore that in-between thing that sits in the unstable balance between pure abstraction and market value.

On the other hand, not all inventions are equal. In particular, most inventions are incremental (like the ones that came to mind while I was looking for examples for my cousins). That is to say they consist of small improvements to an already known product or method. They are usually born in the minds of skilled persons who are familiar with the state of the art and identify a gap in traditional techniques that needs to be filled. Such inventions are legion in the intellectual assets of companies because they fit perfectly into their traditional field of activity. In contrast, so-called radical inventions are of a completely different nature, since they shake up the established order and propose solutions that depart from conventions. This is why they often come from players from different fields, who traditional companies did not otherwise consider to be their competitors. These inventions, which, once transformed into innovations, have the potential to completely reorganize or "disrupt" the market, do however make relatively rare appearances.

The second difficulty mentioned above, which proves greater than the first one, relates to the very purpose of the patent. Unlike the invention it is supposed to protect, the patent is a less familiar phenomenon that is not easily encoded in the way we ordinarily think. What is it really? A legal title? An economic tool? A piece of property? Why is it limited to a certain period of time? Is a patent a monopoly? Then how come patent holders are not always leaders on their market? Is it an exclusive right to practice? If so, why is a patentee not always allowed to use their own invention?

In addition to these difficult questions, there are other equally delicate ones when one considers the objectives the patent supposedly serves. Is it to recognize the parentage of an invention? To reward an intellectual effort? To enable the diffusion of knowledge? To encourage innovation by offering the prospect of extra profit in compensation for prior risky investments in research? In this latter case, how can it be explained that innovation exists and is sometimes vibrant even outside the patent system?

As I progressed in my career, first in a patent law firm and then in a U.S. consumer electronics company with a strong research and development focus, and as I became more familiar with the techniques and uses of patents, these questions began to haunt me. I questioned the theory I had learned during my training. I asked myself about the underlying reason for certain legal provisions or the origins of a particular characteristic of the patent.

In my quest for answers, I discovered that, unlike inventions, the patent was not something that had been around forever. It was a relatively recent construction that was initially only present in particularly advanced societies. Moreover, until recently, patents varied considerably from one country to another, both in their form and in their justifications.

I finally came to the conclusion that to truly understand the current patent system, it was necessary to examine the past and learn about the winding road that has brought us to where we are today. This fascinating story is the subject of the first part of this book, and I have chosen to relay it in the style of narrative storytelling. However, the profile of the patent would not be complete without mention of the most recent challenges it faces. These are discussed in the second part of the book.

The classic training courses to become a patent engineer or an intellectual property attorney focus on the purely technical and legal aspects of the subject. In my opinion, they lack a perspective that would enable young professionals not only to know how to read, write and enforce patents, but also to better understand the spirit of the laws, how approaches vary between different countries and the macroscopic effects of patents on our societies.

My now two decades of questioning and experience in this field have enabled me to gain a little insight into the subject. Given the increasing importance of inventions and innovations in our lives in recent years, and despite my not being an historian or an economist, I thought that my perspective as a patent practitioner could be of benefit to other professionals, enthusiasts or people who are simply curious about the foundations of one of the main engines of our modern economies. I hope that the reader will enjoy reading this book as much as I enjoyed writing it.

One last thing before going back in time. Complete neutrality is not of this world. Even if I have tried to be as factual and objective as possible in my presentation, it would be unrealistic to claim to have achieved total impartiality. The choice of my sources, my inspirations as well as my personal experience may have influenced some of my remarks, in spite of myself. The patent can be, in some respects, a divisive topic that is subject to ideological sway. If some aspects of my text might offend anyone's sensitivity, I apologize in advance. Debating ideas makes the world a better place.

PART 1

A (NEW AND INVENTIVE) HISTORY OF THE PATENT

A LAW EMERGES FROM THE LAGOON

ITALY

Jules Férat, "Le doge de Venise visitant les verreries de Murano",
("The doge of Venice visits the glassworks of Murano")
engraving from the book by Louis Figuier *Les merveilles de l'industrie, ou Description des principales industries modernes*,
Furne, Jouvet & Cie, 1873-1877

A VERY OPAQUE GLASS

THE 14TH CENTURY

It is already late afternoon, Giorgio's favorite time of the day. He sits down by the water and lets the fresh air sting his red cheeks. From the Murano Island, which he knows so well for having worked there all his life like his father and grandfather before him, he contemplates the swell as it reflects the last rays of the sun. He cannot help but feel proud of the idea that, despite its modest size, the city-state of Venice has become a powerful commercial and maritime empire, perhaps even the heart of the world. And his satisfaction is all the greater because he feels he is contributing to this exceptional success.

Giorgio is a master craftsman. He is one of the fieroli *making the famous Venetian glass, the purity and resistance of which have no equivalent in the whole of Europe! Obtaining this valued glass requires a subtle blend of know-how and skills. Its composition includes materials superior to those of Northern European glass. The use of sodium carbonate, in particular, is a major factor in the quality and brilliance of this Venetian product. Northern glassmakers still have not understood this and insist on using potash!*

Giorgio practices his art in a guild: a community of glassmakers, but also a very closed circle that, under the protection of the municipality of Venice, organizes all the activity of its members and the training of apprentices. It is even coupled with a scuola, *a religious confraternity.*

To be part of the guild is a major opportunity, even if life in there is not always easy. Everything is terribly regulated; every action must respect the established norms and the hierarchy is very strict. Fortunately, Giorgio benefits from the authority of the master over the apprentices he trains the less skilled workers who assist him without any hope of becoming full members of the guild.

As the evening sun shows its last rays, Giorgio lets his mind wander to the rhythm of the waves. He is suddenly stopped in his thinking by a coughing fit. The same bad cough that his father and grandfather had developed from inhaling the hot air from the glass furnace. Giorgio is even sure of this: the work of glass took them to their early deaths.

"What if I stopped everything...", thinks Giorgio. Why not run away from Venice and start a new life to escape an unfortunate fate? But is this reasonable? Despite his great talent in glass making, Giorgio does not feel capable of doing any other job. In any case, the guild would not let him go. This would be totally against the rules. It is out of the question that a guild member of Giorgio's quality, with his precise knowledge of the composition and manufacture of glass, could leave Venice. This would jeopardize the whole edifice of secrecy patiently built up by the guild over the years. If the secret were to fall, the entire guild could fall with it. Soon glass of the same quality would be produced in other cities and would compete with the Venetian market. Venetian glass would lose its appeal and its market value would plummet. No, this is simply unthinkable!

It is also out of the question for Giorgio to do what some of his friends did in the past, that is, breaking their oath and trying to leave the guild to practice elsewhere without permission. Giorgio knows what happened to these defectors. They were not left in peace. At best, they were ordered to return within two months. Others were sentenced to pay a heavy fine. Still others were banished outright. No one can ignore these sanctions, which have become more and more severe over the years. The members of the guild are reminded of them regularly, and they are even declaimed to the public in the San Marco and Rialto districts.

"In any event," Giorgio thinks, "I care too much about the group to be able to leave it. And I also have to perpetuate the family tradition. What would my father and grandfather think if I turned my back on the path they set for me? Perhaps I will even have the chance to see my son take up the torch and contribute, in turn, to the collective task that makes our city great..."

With its gentle caresses, the evening air finally calms Giorgio's cheeks and breathing, as well as his thoughts. Looking at the horizon, Giorgio now only dreams of a good night's sleep. Tomorrow at dawn, the devouring fire of the furnaces will once again replace the quiet silence of the water.

*

While Giorgio is a fictional character, the description of the guild in charge of making Venetian glass is based on historical facts.

The guild is a form of organization that became the norm around the 12th and 13th centuries in the medieval cities of Italy and elsewhere in Europe. Beyond glass, guilds developed and operated in many craft sectors such as wool, silk or woodworking. The state gave them exclusive rights to operate in their field, so that no one could practice the same trades outside the guild without its approval. This was especially true for foreigners, who were usually not allowed to join.

As collective organizations, guilds gathered know-how in the hands of their members. This system was based on the strict protection of know-how through secrecy. The strict regulations of the guilds were largely aimed at ensuring this secrecy: if a secret were to fall into the hands of third parties, this could indeed have led to a depreciation of the commercial value of the manufactured products. It was therefore crucial that members were not allowed to leave the guild.

By giving such great importance to the protection of manufacturing techniques and other kinds of know-how, guilds laid the foundations of intellectual property (without yet using this much more recent expression). Indeed, these skills were intangible elements, separate from the real, material craft products which were intended to be sold to as many people as possible. The awareness that intangible things, distinct from that of the final products, had a value on their own that was worthy of protection corresponded to a change in attitude towards knowledge. As such, a proprietary attitude based on secrecy was born.

This model, which preceded that of patents, prompts us to think about the forms that markets could take in the absence of systems for protecting intellectual property. It suggests that in the absence of specific legislation, corporations such as guilds can naturally emerge to preserve the interests of small groups of individuals and ensure, through strict regulation, the means of their perpetuation.

It would take the audacity and genius of ambitious individuals to emancipate themselves from the omnipotence of the guilds.

Dredging machine designed by Leonardo da Vinci (1452-1519)

Would it be inspired by Brunelleschi's barge?

Source: Drawing by Michael,
inspired by a sketch from Manuscrit E of Leonardo da Vinci
kept at the Institut de France

THE GENIE IS OUT OF THE BOTTLE

FILIPPO BRUNELLESCHI, 1421

It is a heartbreaking sight. Filippo Brunelleschi, who is not normally one to complain, cannot repress his tears. The titanic work of several years, not to say of a lifetime, is collapsing before his eyes!

The sight is that of Brunelleschi's ship sinking on its first trip. And with it, a good part of Brunelleschi's personal fortune disappears into the depths of the river.

Yet this boat was Filippo's greatest pride. He had conceived it by the sheer force of his mind to be a barge capable of transporting blocks of marble down the Arno River, all the way from the mountains of Carrara to the heart of Florence.

Brunelleschi, the famous architect who has succeeded in everything up to this point, has difficulty accepting this failure. After all, he was the one entrusted with the construction of a huge octagonal dome for the Opera del Duomo, *the great cathedral of Florence. For this unusual project, he had to be very creative: he dispensed with the traditional rigid wooden scaffolding and* designed his own lifting crane to transport building materials more quickly and safely. It was also for this construction site that he had created his barge...

As he watches his beloved ship sink, Brunelleschi cannot help but think of all the battles he had to fight to get there. He had to fight against the ruthless guild of wood and stone workers, who wanted to take away ownership of his inventions. Yet he, and he alone, is the inventor of his construction devices and methods! He had already made up his mind long ago: he would never join the guild and he would never give up his wonderful inventions.

That is why, relying on his ingenuity, Brunelleschi had asked the city of Florence for a privilege, a special right, concerning the invention of his barge. In his application, he said he would refuse to make his invention public to prevent the fruit of his genius from being stolen. He would only reveal what he had kept secret if he was given privileges over his invention.

His courage had finally paid off; the municipality had granted him an exclusive right for three years to manufacture and sail his boat on Florentine waters. Now, Brunelleschi sees the very same boat sinking before his eyes before he has been able to take advantage of even a little of his privilege.

Filippo closes his eyes and takes a deep breath. As he comes to his senses, he feels gradually filled up with an unexpected serenity. His ship may be lost forever, but Brunelleschi suddenly understands that his genius, his most precious asset, will survive.

*

The exclusive right granted to the architect Filippo Brunelleschi (1377-1446) by the city of Florence in 1421 is sometimes considered the first patent in history. However, it was not the first monopoly granted over an invention.

Earlier examples have been reported, starting in ancient times. The earliest surviving reference is probably that attributed to the historian Phylarchus of the city of Sybaris, a Greek colony in Calabria, as early as the 3rd century B.C. It is said to have been the custom of this city to grant protection for one year to cooks who had invented a particularly original and tasty dish. This practice seems to have disappeared with the destruction of the city without being adopted elsewhere in the ancient world.

Other examples followed in the Middle Ages in the particular form of royal privileges, which will be discussed in more detail in subsequent chapters. At this point, let us simply say that such privileges were classic tools used to grant particular rights to individuals in exchange for services rendered to the crown or deemed useful to society. In the 15th century, however, privileges were only used in sporadic and isolated cases to protect craft activities or inventions.

The case of Brunelleschi is remarkable in several respects. First, the way the architect systematically and frontally opposed the guilds was highly unusual. This confrontation even led to his being imprisoned for 11 days! As we have seen, the guilds exercised tight control over certain trades and fields of activity. It follows that they should not be pleased with the rebellious attitude of a competitor like Brunelleschi who refused to join them. Given the influence of the guilds, an individual – even if they were well educated and came from a family of lawyers, like Brunelleschi – had to show courage to dare to fight against them.

The second element of interest lies in the justification Brunelleschi put forward to obtain a privilege, namely his ingenuity. Guilds derived their prerogatives from the collective expertise of their members, which were transmitted orally from generation to generation through apprenticeships. Inventions were probably made from time to time within the guilds, but it is likely that this happened in an understated manner without the origin of these inventions necessarily being linked to a particular individual. By relying on his genius to claim a privilege, Brunelleschi made a causal link between the personal origin of his invention and the exclusive right that derives from it, which was a departure from the usual way in which guilds operated.

Finally, Brunelleschi could have mimicked the guild system and concealed the details of his invention as he had initially threatened to do. Since the invention was about a device (the barge), this would probably not have prevented the guilds from analyzing and reproducing it. In the end, the architect opted for disclosure, which is the opposite of the principle of secrecy on which the guilds' model was based. Logically, he made the public availability of his invention conditional on obtaining an exclusive right to use it, a necessary condition to avoid competition from the guilds through imitation.

If the medieval urban model of the guild was a key factor in the emergence of intellectual property, it is paradoxically the emancipation from these same guilds that made it shift closer to what was later to become the patent. This emancipation was made possible, in particular, by the courage and self-confidence of Filippo Brunelleschi. In this respect, the recognition of the genius of artists that began with the Italian Renaissance offered a particularly favorable context for the architect's claims.

Florence had just reached an important milestone in the development of the patent. But the weight and greatness of Venice were necessary conduits behind the next and more important step.

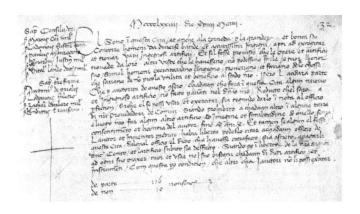

Text of the *Parte Veneziana*

Source: Extract from the state archives of Venice -
www.archiviodistatovenezia.it -
Public domain

Secrecy Takes on Water

Parte Veneziana, 1474

Let us go back to Venice, now in the 15th century.

The well-known case of Brunelleschi is not unique, nor is it limited to Florence. Similar privileges were granted to other individuals and in other places. This was especially the case in Venice. As the city-state grew in importance and opened up to the world, its development policy changed. Venice became aware of the economic and social interest of creating and promoting new industries and commercial activities. To this end, it needed to attract skilled workers, which it did by granting foreigners various legal, fiscal and social advantages (cancellation of debts, judicial immunity, etc.) in exchange for moving their operations to the city.

In this context, the guilds and their tight controls over entire technical fields began to be perceived as a hindrance to the development of the city. The incentive to immigrate to Venice to create new industries was indeed insufficient for foreign entrepreneurs, who knew that the powerful guilds would compete with them and perhaps even appropriate their inventions. The idea therefore gradually took hold that talented people from abroad should be granted exclusive rights to operate in the city, even if this might harm its established guilds. Privileges became the instrument of this policy. An increasing number of titles similar to Brunelleschi's were granted for activities or inventions deemed useful to society. For example, a privilege was granted in 1470 for the making of glassware "in the manner of Sudan".

By 1474, this use of privileges was developed enough to become one of the official means of Venice's industrialization policy. The Venetian Senate decided to codify the practice and voted, by a majority of 116 to 10 (with 3 abstentions), in favor of a short text that marked a milestone in the story of the patent. This text, known as the *Parte Veneziana*, is the first known legislation on patents. It legally established the principle of granting an exclusive right of exploitation to inventors (including importers).

The strength of this text laid precisely in its status as a law, which gave it a more general and objective scope than the prior practice whereby privileges were granted on an occasional and individual basis.

This law granted inventors a 10-year monopoly over their inventions. During the term of protection, no one (including the guilds) could reproduce the invention under penalty of a fine and the destruction of the infringing products. If the invention was not used, however, the Senate could withdraw the privilege from its holder.

Criteria had to be met before inventors could benefit from such protection. The invention – the object of the monopoly – had to have been:

- useful to society: as we have seen, this was the main motivation for the authorities to grant privileges as part of their economic development policy for the city;

- new: this referred to a "relative" novelty within the limits of the Venetian territory only. This limitation was what allowed foreigners to import techniques and skills that were already practiced elsewhere into Venice; and

-   ingenious: this criterion was reminiscent of the reason put forward by Brunelleschi to justify his privilege. It can be considered the ancestor of the more recent notions of "inventive activity" or "non-obviousness".

By democratizing inventions and institutionalizing a right that created competition for their activities, the *Parte Veneziana* must have triggered the anger of the guilds. It seems, moreover, that the guilds proactively ensured that the authorities did not grant monopolies on certain inventions, alleging their lack of novelty or ingenuity. This can be seen as a primitive form of the opposition procedure that is well known today, whereby a patent is invalidated if it does not meet the necessary conditions and should therefore not have been granted. In this respect, it is interesting to note that the ingenuity criterion was not taken up as such in the legislation that followed in other countries. One can therefore assume that its use in Venice can be explained by a desire of the authorities to preserve the guilds by not granting monopolies to third parties which might have overlapped with too much of their activities.

In the wake of the individual privileges granted in the 15th century, the system laid out by the *Parte Veneziana* was strikingly modern and broke with the prior model of the guilds. It in fact represents the shift from a tradition of keeping secrets within a closed community to the reign of publicly claimed individual genius. It also marks an essential change in the terms of protection. Rights that were once perpetual (as long as the members of a guild are faithful to it) became limited to fixed periods of time.

The model created in Venice was therefore a major step towards the patent systems we know today. However, it features some important differences from our current conceptions that should not be overlooked. One in particular lies in the dual character of the Venetian patent. In addition to the exclusivity it granted vis-à-vis third parties, this patent also gave its beneficiary a right to operate their invention. This was a necessary condition for inventors to be able to practice their activity outside of the guilds. However, this dimension of the patent, which favors competition between players in the same sector, has been lost today, resulting in "blocking" situations between holders of dependent patents – a phenomenon that will be explained later.

The *Parte Veneziana* was a real success and indeed made Venice attractive to many foreign entrepreneurs. However, despite its innovative character, it was not replicated in Florence or in other Italian cities; it even fell little by little into oblivion. The ideas that it sowed in the ingenious minds of inventors would nevertheless later spread to other countries.

FROM ROYAL PRIVILEGE
TO PATENT

WHEN THE COMMON LAW GETS INVOLVED

ENGLAND

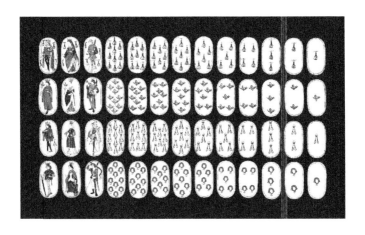

The oldest complete set of ordinary playing cards

It comes from the south of the Netherlands at the end of the 15th century.
Did Edward Darcy's cards look like these?

A LOSING CARD GAME

Darcy v. Allen, 1603

"It was time for this litigation to finally end," says Edward Coke to himself. The case had been extremely stressful for him, and the facts discussed before the common law court were unusual, almost caricature. But Coke knows that the decision will be far-reaching, beyond what the parties can even imagine. "This is, in a way, the Case of Monopolies," he thinks.

As he learns the outcome of the case, Coke feels conflicting emotions. Being the current Attorney General, he found himself forced to defend Edward Darcy and, in order to do so, he has had to put aside his personal views. A lawyer of his caliber – probably the best in England – is not a man to shirk his responsibilities! Professionalism must come before political ideas, and as he is never half-hearted in his approach, he took his role seriously and put all his elegance, natural authority and charisma to the service of the plaintiff, Darcy.

But in this case, his exceptional ability to hypnotize judges, witnesses and opposing counsels to achieve his aims was not enough to win for Darcy.

"Obviously", he thinks, "Darcy's case could not be won. That this favorite of Queen Elizabeth I obtained a letters patent in 1598 giving him an exclusive right to manufacture, import and sell playing cards was already highly questionable. Did he really need to put this exclusivity into effect and sue Thomas Allen to prevent him from importing his own cards into England?!"

It is somewhat ironic that he, Coke, has had to find arguments to justify Darcy's rights given his hostility to monopolies and their negative consequences on the business and employment of the kingdom's craftsmen! Moreover, Darcy's monopoly was clearly abusive and counter to practice, as it was granted while playing cards were already widespread in England.

Could anyone reasonably imagine an outcome to the dispute other than the invalidation of Darcy's monopoly? Coke's mind wanders: "What if the outcome had been different... would I have been blamed for supporting this odious monopoly?" He prefers not to think about it.

Coke sits down and mentally goes over the various points of the judgment one by one. One particular point catches his attention: a monopoly must not have the effect of preventing merchants from continuing carrying on their current business. This is especially relevant in Darcy's case, as Darcy has simply no expertise in the field of playing cards. This idea sends him once more into deep contemplation.

No, Coke can definitely not take offense to this decision. If the court had ruled otherwise, it would have set a dangerous precedent, calling into question many useful activities in the kingdom, resulting in job losses and unjustified price increases.

Coke now feels totally relieved. He played his role as Attorney General well and upheld professional behavior. From now on, he thinks, he will use all his strength to prevent any more unworthy monopolies from being created.

Before the famous *Darcy v. Allen* case, which was decided in 1603, the English crown had already granted royal privileges for inventions. These privileges were given in the form of "*litterae patentes*", or letters patents. The latter got their name from the fact that, unlike "*litterae clausae*", which were sealed and closed to public inspection, letters patents remained open so that their content was exposed to public view. This instrument was used by the sovereign to allocate parts of the public domain to private parties. It was not limited to inventions and could involve the granting of offices, franchises or other privileges. And when letters patents were granted for an invention, they did not necessarily confer a monopoly on its holder, but could be limited to granting them the mere right of use on their invention.

The first English letters patents date from the 14th century during the reign of King Edward III (1312-1377). Like in Venice, their main purpose was to attract foreigners to settle in the kingdom, practice their trades and train apprentices. The patents thus acted, in a way, as passports. The first recipient of such a patent in England may have been a Flemish weaver named John Kempe in 1331.

A century later, in 1449, a patent was granted to another Flemish artist, John of Utynam, who came to England at the request of King Henry VI (1421-1471) to produce stained glass windows. This time, however, the right granted to Utynam consisted an actual monopoly on the manufacture of the stained glass windows for a period of 20 years (which is not unlike the current term of patent protection).

The case of Utynam appears to be isolated. It was not until the 16th century that the crown more regularly issued letters patents granting monopolies over manufacturing.

Thus, the young King Edward VI (1537-1553) granted to a man named Henry Smyth a letters patent providing a monopoly on the production of Normandy glass in 1552 that also lasted for 20 years. In exchange for this monopoly, Smyth agreed to 1) operate his techniques in the kingdom, 2) not harm citizens and existing industries, and 3) train apprentices in such a way as to create a self-sustaining local industry.

These three conditions clearly show that the letters patent of the time was a tool intended to support the royal economic policies, in keeping with a clear mercantilist agenda that promoted trade and the accumulation of wealth through the export of manufactured goods and the limitation of imports.

During her reign, Queen Elizabeth I (1533-1603) also used her royal prerogative to issue letters patents. In continuity with her predecessors, she granted monopolies that followed the same standard as shown in Smyth's case. In particular, by virtue of the second condition set out above, these monopolies could only relate to inventions (including imports) that were not already the subject of a previously established industry in the kingdom (or had disappeared from the kingdom for a long enough period time), so as not to harm employment.

Soon after, however, the Queen began to abuse her prerogative. She soon granted letters patents for the sole purpose of rewarding her favorites for their loyalty and filling the state coffers. The resulting monopolies were particularly problematic, covering not only the manufacture but also the sale of products. In addition, the three above-mentioned conditions for granting monopolies were no longer met, especially the one intended to protect existing industries. The granting of abusive monopolies led to the immediate prohibition of trade in certain common goods, such as salt, vinegar, starch, paper and... playing cards.

Feeling their interests threatened by arbitrarily granted monopolies, the urban bourgeoisie and the guilds lobbied the Parliament to restrict the royal prerogative. Litigation over letters patents was entrusted, at least in part, to the common law courts. It is in this context of tension between powers that the lawsuit initiated by Edward Darcy took place.

By declaring Darcy's monopoly invalid under the common law and by reaffirming the previously existing conditions for the granting of letters patents, the Case of Monopolies – as Edward Coke called it – provided a much-needed clarification. It did not, however, call into question the fundamental idea that patents were instruments of royal prerogative intended to support economic policies decided by the crown.

Even in a country like England, where, unlike Roman law, the law is more contentious and empirical than prescriptive, and where case law and precedents have legal authority, the judgment in *Darcy v. Allen* was not enough to put things right. The full force of the law was needed to finally restore order in the practices.

Sir Edward Coke (1552-1634) painted by an unknown artist

A PRIVILEGED MONOPOLY

STATUTE OF MONOPOLIES, 1623

After the case *Darcy v. Allen*, King James (1603-1625) took the crown. Despite his more open rhetoric, he too abused his prerogative of issuing letters patents that granted unfair monopolies. The conflict between the royal power and the Parliament became more and more serious, and it was not until 1623 that Parliament finally passed the law known as the "Statute of Monopolies". The text was drafted by Sir Edward Coke – the man we met in the Darcy case – who had then become a parliamentarian. King James had no choice but to reluctantly approve the law.

What is the content of the Statute of Monopolies? This short piece of legislation declared all monopolies to be against the law of the land and therefore abrogated all those that had previously been granted. One important exception was nevertheless provided for: the crown could still grant monopolies for "any manner of new manufacture", and only to the "first and true inventor" – i.e. the person who had actually introduced the invention into the kingdom, whether by invention or by importation.

For monopolies on inventions, the Statute reiterated the same doctrinal conditions as those already set forth in the case of Henry Smyth almost a century earlier. For example, this included the requirement for any manufacture to be new. The condition of relative novelty was intended to protect industries already established in the kingdom. For the same reasons, the granting of a monopoly on an invention that improved an existing manufacture was prohibited. The absence of an increase in selling prices or of other effects that may be detrimental to the trade or the state remained a necessary condition for the issuance of patents under the new law.

As far as inventions were concerned, the Statute of Monopolies did not therefore constitute a break with previous practice. It did, however, include some legal innovations. In particular, a significant contribution of the new law consisted in setting a fixed duration for the patents, whereas the monopolies granted previously featured different durations depending on the utility of the inventions or the goodwill of the king. The term selected by the law was 14 years, which corresponded to two successive 7-year apprenticeship cycles, that is to say, more or less one generation of craftsmen. In this way, the inventor could enjoy their monopoly without facing competition from their own apprentices.

While being a continuation of prior practice, the Statute afforded the force of law to the Parliament's long-standing desire to limit the royal power of issuing letters patents. By handing over the fate of monopolies to the common law, it aimed to eliminate any arbitrary element in the granting of patents. Moreover, by reserving monopolies to "true" inventors, it initiated a subtle shift from royal economic opportunism to the protection of inventive effort.

Nowadays, patents are sometimes seen as excessive impediments to individual freedom of trade. It is therefore worth remembering that in England, they emerged not from a strengthening, but from a limitation of the royal power to grant overly broad monopolies. They derived not from an extension of the power to arbitrarily grant monopolies, but rather from a recognition of the specificity of the inventor's work.

In practice, the coming into force of the Statute of Monopolies in 1624 did not fundamentally change the situation and the crown continued to issue abusive monopolies, bringing the institution into disrepute. The letters patent system was put on hold for about twenty years before being re-introduced in 1660 under the reign of King James II (1633-1701). The latter was more cautious than his predecessors, in such a way that, unlike in the rest of Europe at the time, English patents were soon no longer perceived as instruments of the mercantilist policy of the royal power.

The number of patents issued each year in the decades following the Statute of Monopolies remained small, although higher than elsewhere in Europe. Indeed, several essential elements were still missing for inventors to take up the system. Nevertheless, with the Statute, the oldest continuing patent system in the world was born.

Shire Hall in Chelmsford,
built by the architect John Johnson at the end of the 18th century

Engraving from *The Eastern Counties Railway Illustrated Guide*, 1851,
available at the British Library in London

A DESCRIPTION FROM THE CENTER
OF A BLOODY BATTLE

LIARDET V. JOHNSON, 1780

John Liardet is ecstatic. His long and hard years of legal fight have finally proved successful. In this early July 1780, the jury has just ordered a definitive ban against his rival, John Johnson!

Liardet, a Protestant clergyman born in Lausanne, Switzerland, has thus come to defeat Johnson, the London based and Leicester born architect. He had serious doubts about his ability to win, as he understands English poorly and had to call on a friend of his wife to help him with his legal proceedings. If there were one thing, however, that he was sure of, it was his inventive genius. He knew that the time he had invested in his research would eventually pay off. And when he obtained a patent for a stucco using a special cement in 1773, he had the intuition that his invention would bring him big money.

It is true that he had to enter into a partnership with four architects – the Adam brothers – because he is a man of ideas and abstraction with no business experience. He even had to assign his patent to them before taking it back in order to obtain an extension of its term from 14 to 18 years from the Parliament. From the start, he had had the feeling that this alliance would be a source of future problems. But did he really have a choice?

The need to submit a description of his invention to obtain a patent had posed a moral dilemma to him, as he feared that such a piece of writing would enable a third party to reproduce his stucco too easily without his authorization. When he learned that John Johnson was using the composition of his invention, it seemed obvious to him that his competitor had managed to get hold of his description and reproduce its subject — perhaps with the help of one of the Adam brothers...

Liardet's lawsuit against Johnson, which was started in 1777 to seek compensation and an injunction on his stucco, had been a major ordeal. Not one, but two trials had to be conducted, due to allegations that the judge, Lord Mansfield, showed bias in his favor. The second hearing of July 1778 lasted no less than 14 hours! No doubt there was something extraordinary about his case.

The defense had spared no effort nor argument. Johnson had dared to claim that his composition was different from that of Liardet, since it contained blood serum. "Blood, is that all?! It is Johnson's blood that should be flowing for his offense to me," Liardet had raged. Fortunately, the scientific expert, appearing as a witness, had foiled the trickery and demonstrated that the two compositions were more or less the same, with Johnson's blood serum proving to be a totally useless addition.

But that was not all. Johnson had also questioned the validity of Liardet's patent on the grounds that the stucco composition would not only not be new, but that it would also be insufficiently described to enable other craftsmen to use it! The defense had made extensive efforts to substantiate its allegations.

It had presented a whole array of books, dictionaries and other prior art documents in an attempt to locate Liardet's cement in prior usage. Luckily, all the known compositions were missing at least one element: sand, lead or drying agent.

John Liardet shuddered as he heard Lord Mansfield repeat Johnson's various points and rephrase them as questions to the members of the jury.

Today, as he learns that the jury has ruled in his favor and granted his request for an injunction against Johnson, Liardet almost forgets all the inconvenience that these years of trials have caused him. He thanks God for having endowed him with a mind that is not only inventive, but also combative. And he feels indebted to the justice of his adopted country, which was able to recognize his genius and protect the fruit of his efforts.

*

Until the beginning of the 17th century, letters patents were the instrument of the king's mercantilist policy to develop self-sufficient local industry. By emphasizing the singularity of the "first and true inventor" and the need for inventions to be new, the Statute of Monopolies of 1623 initiated a paradigm shift. However, the Privy Council – the body responsible for advising the English monarch – refused to relinquish its jurisdiction over patent disputes, a field it still considered a royal prerogative until the beginning of the 18th century.

It was not until 1753, 130 years after the Statute, that the common law courts were finally recognized as the sole competent jurisdiction to judge the validity of patents. This represented a major change and completed the transfer of patents from the domain of the king to that of civil society. The patent thus went from being a favor granted by the

45

crown to a contract between an inventor and society as a whole. This shift gave the courts much greater leeway, since invalidating an inventor's right to their invention was infinitely easier than challenging a privilege granted by the king himself.

This evolution resulted in changes in the way patents were granted and assessed for validity. One of these changes consisted in requiring a detailed description of the invention that was the subject of the patent, known as a "specification". It is true that a few (rare) descriptions had been presented by inventors previously; the first known one was submitted in 1611, and the second exactly one century later. These were however offered on a voluntary basis. Submitting a specification was much more frequent thereafter, becoming common practice from 1734 onwards.

The case *Liardet v. Johnson* took place in this context. The need for Liardet to submit a description of his composition was the standard of the 18th century. However, where the judge Lord Mansfield seems to have innovated (as shown by the way he phrased his questions to the jury) was in making the validity of the patent conditional on the sufficiency of the description, i.e. the ability of the specification to allow the invention to be reproduced.

With the introduction of the "sufficiency of description" criterion in the English system in the 18th century, the specification became the object of consideration for the granting of a patent. It thus replaced the previous requirement that inventions be operated in the kingdom.

Today, practitioners around the world are familiar with the sufficient disclosure requirement that now exists in all patent laws. They certainly understand Liardet's dilemma, given the difficulty of providing enough material to meet the requirement without disclosing superfluous information that would help third parties infringe the patented invention.

The *Liardet v. Johnson* case is also interesting from another standpoint: that of the concept of novelty. We have seen previously that the novelty required at the time of Queen Elizabeth I was relative, that is to say that the granting of a royal privilege on an invention or on imported industry should not prevent craftsmen in the kingdom from practicing their pre-existing activity. The Statute of Monopolies began to change the situation by linking the concept of novelty to the first and true inventor only. The importer into England of a technique already known and implemented abroad could not legitimately be called the first and true inventor. Thus, the novelty standard changed to become absolute at the end of the 18th century. In order to give rise to a patent, an invention must have henceforth been totally new, unknown in England as elsewhere.

This is reflected in the novelty analysis in *Liardet v. Johnson*. The various prior publications cited by the defense were submitted in an unsuccessful attempt to prove that Liardet's composition was already known by persons skilled in the art of cementing. The test that Lord Mansfield applied in this case was thus consistent with the modern concept of absolute novelty. At the same time, the original concept of utility lost its importance as the market became the ultimate decision-maker in determining which inventions were worth operating.

The introduction of the sufficient disclosure requirement and the emergence of the absolute novelty concept illustrate the extent of the changes that took place in the English patent system during the 18th century. While there were many economic, political and social reasons for these changes, one reason was undoubtedly moral.

At least this is the convincing theory made by law Professor Adam Mossoff. He argues that 18th century judges, like Lord Mansfield, were relatively free at the time and adopted a new conception of patents inspired by John Locke's philosophy of natural rights (even though the

17th century philosopher never directly addressed the subject of inventions). According to this conception, inventors had a natural right to dispose of the fruits of their intellectual labor, and the patent was the appropriate tool to guarantee this right.

By definitively leaving its status of royal privilege and pivoting towards something close to a legal contract between the inventor and society at the end of the 18th century, the patent thus changed in nature and objective. It became a powerful tool for the promotion and protection of inventions, of which English inventors would henceforth take full advantage. This change came at the perfect time to support the first Industrial Revolution and, along with the steam engine, to propel England to the forefront of global technological development.

Was this transformation too rapid, or was it misunderstood? In any case, the patent was to simultaneously provoke growing enthusiasm among some and growing hostility among others.

Illustration of the short story by Charles Dickens,
A Poor Man's Tale of a Patent, edition of 1900

OLD JOHN, AN UNHAPPY GENIUS

CHARLES DICKENS, 1850

At the age of 56, John, nicknamed "Old John" because of his premature baldness, is bitter. So much so that he has decided to take up his pen to tell the world about the injustice he has just suffered.

He has spent his entire life working as a blacksmith in his Birmingham workshop. Over twenty years, he has developed and perfected an invention of ingenious nature. As such, both he and his wife felt strongly when, on Christmas Eve, they came together to contemplate the model that embodied so many years of effort and dedication. They could not hold back tears of joy.

This quantity of work deserved to be recognized. John decided to apply for a patent on his invention, despite the advice of his friend, William Butcher, who had tried to dissuade him. John had a nice amount of money that his wife had inherited. What better use could be made of these funds?

John went to London and rented a house from the carpenter Thomas Joy. With Thomas and William's help, he prepared a patent application to Queen Victoria. His years of hard work would soon be rewarded, he thought. However, he had to deal with an unimaginable bureaucratic process, which involved running from one department to another, dealing with a series of strange formalities and draining his money at every step.

As he recounts his misadventure, John still cannot believe it. In the end, he had to go through no less than thirty-five stages, forcing him to stay in London for six weeks and to squander a large part of his inheritance on incomprehensible procedures. And yet, his patent covers England only. A protection extended to the whole United Kingdom would have cost him three times more!

John feels discouraged. William Butcher had warned him from the beginning. Maybe he should have kept his invention for himself...

Still, he has become obsessed with a question: what is the meaning of all this? By making his invention and seeking a patent, John had just thought of making the fruits of his ingenuity available to all, for the common good. How is it then that after having gone through so many difficulties, he now feels guilty, as if he had committed a bad deed?

*

John, the narrator and protagonist of this story, is none other than the main character of Charles Dickens' (1812-1870) short story, *A Poor Man's Tale of a Patent*, published in 1850. Interestingly, the patent became such an integral part of 19th century British culture and society that the greatest novelist of the Victorian era, the father of David Copperfield and Oliver Twist, made it the central theme of one of his works.

Yet the picture Dickens painted is gloomy: the patent is too expensive, and the complexity of its grant procedure is totally absurd. In taking this critical stance, Dickens was in fact belatedly echoing the work of protest movements.

At that time, the Industrial Revolution had already profoundly changed the country. Britain's formerly agrarian and artisanal society was transformed into a predominantly industrial and commercial one. The change was relatively rapid and violent for some, such as the textile craftsmen whose profession was threatened by the development of mechanical looms. These craftsmen tried to resist in the 1810s during the so-called "Luddites" revolt, during which they destroyed many weaving machines. Their efforts were in vain, as their jobs almost disappeared only ten years later. This is a lesson to be learned: technical and economic development is only progress for those who have nothing to lose in the change. Innovation produces winners and losers. As the economist Joseph Schumpeter would later theorize, creation also generates destruction.

On the other hand, the mechanization of British society has caused the number of granted patents to take off. This increase has even more clearly highlighted the archaic nature of the procedures in place.

Dickens' story is deliberately satirical. His exaggeration reaches its peak when Old John claims to have gone through 35 procedural steps. The reality would have been closer to 7 steps in total, which is already substantial! Also, the necessity of having to pay a fee at each step is demonstrated. The total cost of obtaining a patent was indeed prohibitive, reserving the patent to an elite with financial means or political connections.

And yet, the patent was more necessary than ever in an era of increasing foreign competition. Not long before this, Great Britain still regarded the United States as a country unable to match its level of innovation. But by 1808, the number of U.S. patents exceeded the number of English patents. The same happened with French patents in 1817. In 1851, the first universal exhibition, the *Great Exhibition of the Works of Industry of all Nations*, took place in London in the Crystal Palace built for this purpose. This exhibition raised awareness around the need to reform a system that had remained globally unchanged since the Statute of Monopolies and was more than two centuries old!

The first major modification of this patent law took place in 1852. The Statute of Monopolies had strongly influenced the establishment of a patent system in the United States. In a surprising reversal, it was from within the American system that the new English law took on improved elements. In particular, the fees were reduced and the grant procedure was streamlined under a single office, the *Great Seal Patent Office*. However, the latter did not examine inventions based on merit. In the meantime, English patent protection was extended to Scotland and Ireland. A mechanism for maintaining patents in force, based on the payment of fees staggered over time, was introduced. To facilitate access, patents began to be printed and published.

These clear improvements led to an acceleration of patent filing activity, as well as an increase in opportunistic behavior of applicants seeking to block competition rather than promote innovation. The reforms did not succeed in appeasing opposition, notably because of the unpredictable nature of court decisions rendered by judges as well as juries. The assessment of the utility criterion, which remained in the law, seemed particularly arbitrary and disconnected from commercial success.

After an unprecedented wave of liberalism in Europe that was hostile to patents, the reform process resumed. In 1883, a new English patent office was created and proceeded to undertake a summary examination of applications. However, it was not until 1902 that a substantive examination – still limited to the criterion of novelty – appeared, after a report had highlighted the fact that more than 40% of patented inventions had already been disclosed in prior British publications. The law of 1883 was subject to numerous successive revisions throughout the 20th century.

England had been a pioneer in the 17th century, creating a patent system that would support its dazzling technical development during the first Industrial Revolution. Other countries would soon follow the example that England had set for the world.

THE REVOLUTION OF IDEAS

FRANCE

LA GRANDE GALLERIE DE VERSAILLES

Sébastien Leclerc (1637-1714),
View of the Hall of Mirrors at the Palace of Versailles, circa 1684

Broken glass

Antonio still cannot believe it. Was he dreaming? No, since the paper in his hands was just given to him by the great Colbert in person, Comptroller General of Finance and powerful minister of King Louis XIV!

A French clergyman he had met in Venice had promised him that if he agreed to follow him to France, Colbert himself would take care of his establishment. But Antonio had not really paid attention. Why would a minister of Colbert's level be interested in him?

Certainly, Antonio is an extremely talented master glassmaker. A true artist. He is from a family of illustrious glassmakers who have built the reputation of his guild. His ancestor Giorgio, who had contributed to the success of the guild by considerably improving the quality of glass, has been a role model for generations of apprentices. Despite his natural modesty, Antonio knows that he has inherited the gift of his predecessors. He too has made many improvements to glassmaking techniques. His greatest achievement has been to modify the glass blowing technique to produce large cylinders that can be cut lengthwise and then heated, so that they unfold into large flat rectangles. This improvement has allowed production of significantly larger pieces of glass.

This is probably what attracted the attention of France. The clergyman who had sought to meet Antonio had told him that the kingdom was working on a secret project that required the participation of the very best glassmakers. During their brief meeting, which has just ended, Colbert was even more explicit: in 1665, the king created a royal glass factory that he commissioned to a huge gallery in the Baroque style building at the Palace of Versailles, which was to be almost entirely covered with large mirrors. A grandiose project indeed, and one in which a master glassmaker of Antonio's caliber had to participate!

Of course, Antonio is loyal to his country and his guild, whose strict rules he knows all too well. However, what counts most in the world for him is the practice of his art. He believes that it should not be bound by borders, nor prevented by political considerations. For Antonio, art must be guided only by passion.

Antonio had thus had no difficulty in choosing to follow the French envoy. His meeting with Colbert had successfully convinced him to settle in the kingdom of France. It is true that the offer that the minister has just made to him, and which is written clearly on the paper that he holds between his still trembling hands, cannot be refused: France will pay him a high salary and will take care of his housing. Moreover, if his work on the mirrors proves to be up to the expectations of the sovereign, Antonio could be granted French nationality. Colbert even mentioned a possible ennoblement!

Antonio gets dizzy as he repeats to himself the last words pronounced by the minister. How important the project of the great gallery must be for the "Sun King" to send someone out all the way to Venice and offer such conditions to him, Antonio, who had never left his native land before! But on second thought, even more than the promised rewards, it is the prospect of participating in such an extravagant project that dazzles him the most. He has made his decision: tomorrow he will go to Versailles to find Colbert and tell him that he accepts his offer.

In the meantime, he can rest and enjoy the comfortable accommodation at his disposal. He sits down on the soft bench in the middle of his room and pours himself a glass of wine. Perhaps this will help him get rid of the haunting voices of his ancestors that try to dissuade him from leaving his guild. Nonetheless, Antonio has no doubt that he is doing the right thing by serving the King of France. It is not a betrayal, he thinks. On the contrary: by participating in the project of the Great Hall of Mirrors, he will contribute to the perpetuation of a family tradition. How could he better pay tribute to his ancestors than by accepting to put his art at the service of a work that will certainly go down in history?

Antonio is deep in thought when, suddenly, a noise at the door startles him. As he listens, he hears someone say his name and greet him in his native language. Put at ease, he is not suspicious as he opens his door, curious to know if he knows the fellow countryman who has come to visit him. He does not have time to see his face. The mercenary sent by the Venetian guild jumps on Antonio and thrusts a dagger in his heart.

Antonio drops his glass, which breaks, letting the red wine spill on the ground. So, it is the shattering of the glass, this material to which he has dedicated his whole life, which accompanies his last breath of life, he thinks, with a tense smile on his lips.

*

Like his ancestor Giorgio, whom we met earlier in Murano, Antonio is a fictional character. The meeting with Colbert could not have taken place. On the other hand, many elements of this story are taken from reality. Even though several centuries had passed since the great era of Venice when the guilds were still all powerful, they had not disappeared in the 17th century. In fact, efforts to prevent the dissemination of their know-how had only grown stronger. The death penalty was indeed pronounced against several craftsmen who fled their guild, and the murder of several glass workers by Italian mercenaries is historically documented.

Also proven is the role played by Colbert in developing a local glass industry by hiring Italian workers and sending spies to Italy to discover the secret techniques of manufacture. This was the price to pay for the pharaonic project of building the Hall of Mirrors at the Palace of Versailles, through which Louis XIV wanted to make a dazzling demonstration of his power.

To carry out this project, the "Sun King" did create a royal glass manufactory (the origin of the company Saint-Gobain), as reported above. The instrument he used to do so was the royal privilege, exercised in the form of a letters patent. The privilege offered the manufactory a monopoly on the production of mirrors and tax exemptions in exchange for its commitment to develop a new industry in the kingdom. It even went further, imposing predefined dimensions for the produced mirrors and setting a fixed price for their sale. The royal privilege was thus also a tool of regulation at this time.

By contemplating the impressive Hall of Mirrors of the Palace of Versailles today, one can recognize the effectiveness of this royal policy. Moreover, after having acquired the Italian know-how, the glass manufactory gained competence and ended up improving the fabrication processes by itself. It moved from the Venetian technique of blowing to the casting of molten glass on large plates, which considerably increased the surface area of the mirrors. This is a common phenomenon: the acquisition of knowledge is a prerequisite that often leads to innovation. In this case, the innovation was of such importance that it accelerated the decline of Venice as a significant player in glass making.

Combined with close quality control, Colbert's economic policy for encouraging the development of a local industry was reflected in many other fields as well, including textiles and ceramics. Described as "Colbertism", this doctrine was a specific form of mercantilism. If the instrument of this policy was the royal privilege, it was not for the sake of exclusive rights, but because the privilege was then the only tool at hand to achieve the goal of public utility. This tool had indeed been used in relation to inventions for more than a century already. Henry II (1519-1559) granted the first such exclusive privilege in 1551 to Abel Foullon for his invention of the holometer, an instrument used to measure the height of a point above the horizon.

To legitimize the actions of the absolutist state, the privileges of the 17th century were subjected to the rigorous examination of learned societies. The Académie des Sciences, created by Colbert, took on the role of official judge of the novelty and usefulness of inventions in 1699. However, the guilds had the opportunity to oppose the issuance of a royal privilege. France, whose image was still very recently associated with that of a country "without examination" of patents *par excellence* (as we will see later), was thus, in reality, the first to have introduced a strict and systematic examination of inventions!

In the 18th century, however, freedom of trade became a major concern for French society. As a result, exclusive privileges were increasingly criticized, especially since they were the object of growing speculation as businessmen, rather than inventors, increasingly tried to obtain them. In a declaration of 1762, the royal authority tried to better control their use and limit abuses.

Could privileges, like everything associated with absolute monarchy, withstand the revolutionary wave that was soon to hit France?

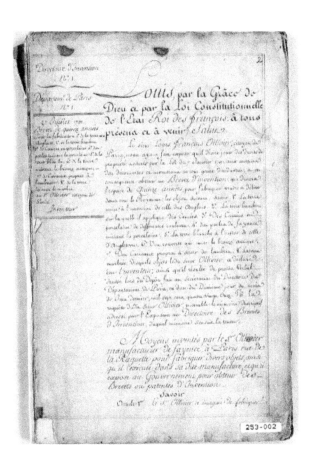

The first French patent,
granted on the 27th of July 1791 to Louis François Ollivier.

The Knight of Thought

Stanislas de Boufflers, 1790

With a quick gesture, the man drops his pen, which rolls across his desk, leaving a few drops of ink in its wake. He leaps to his feet with a worried expression and walks around his room in a disorderly fashion. If he spins around like a caged lion, it is not to warm up on this cold December evening, but rather because he is concerned about the report he must write. His task is tricky and he must mobilize all his intelligence to achieve the goal he has set himself: to convince the Assembly to maintain a protection of inventions that meets the needs of the nation, while distancing from the old privileges whose names have become odious.

He stops dead in the middle of his round and lets out a loud laugh. Would he, the Knight Stanislas de Boufflers, who has seen and experienced almost everything in his 52 years of life, be daunted by the writing of a simple text? He, the literate child of a noble family, who grew up at the court of Lunéville with a former king of Poland as his godfather, who went through the seminary and then, for a longer time, through the army, where he climbed through all the ranks! He even served as governor of Senegal, while smuggling gum arabic and gold, before returning to France, being elected academician and then becoming a deputy of the nobles at the Estates General in 1789. He is used to success, both professional and gallant. It is therefore not a simple report, as delicate as its subject may be, that will get the better of him!

He pulls himself together and returns to his desk. He has made his decision: he will not be satisfied with a timid or lukewarm report. On the contrary, he will be ambitious and will go back to the "principles of the theory". The Knight of Boufflers pauses for a moment to gather his thoughts. He digs in his memory and remembers Diderot's writings on the book trade, which emphasized the close link between the author and their work. He takes his pen once again and writes: "If there is one true property for a man, it is his thought". The emphatic statement delights him. Who would dare to argue with it? Anticipating a possible challenge to the singular nature of the field of technology, he continues: "The invention, that is the source of arts, is also the source of property; it is the primitive property, all the others are conventions".

The Knight is aware of the boldness of his argument. Never before had a law on inventions stated the principle of full and complete ownership in such a clear and general manner! However, he also knows that framing the protection of inventions entirely as a natural right of the inventor is fraught with consequences and is potentially a source of contradiction. In order to guarantee the application of this right, he frames it with something like a contract between the inventor and society. In exchange for the recognition of their property, the inventor must disclose their invention to society and accept the temporary nature of their right.

Boufflers is now totally convinced that recourse to natural law and social contract is the only way to make the whole thing stand.

It will free inventors from the critical eye of the learned societies and the administration, which are incapable of assessing the utility of their inventions early on. The abolition of the preliminary examination and its arbitrary character will give the public and the market the means to judge for themselves the interest of inventions without harming either the inventors or the public authorities.

Satisfied with his reasoning, the Knight of Boufflers still wonders... Will his subtle construction be enough to convince the revolutionaries? Certainly, the bourgeoisie still very much care about the notion of property, but will the deputies not see in his report a way to maintain the privileges of the Ancien Régime? *To reduce this risk, the witty man knows that he must go even further.*

He takes up his pen one last time and, emphasizing the superiority of English laws, he cleverly advocates to follow the example of the Americans who chose to abide them. Attempting to draw an unbridgeable separation from the royal heritage of the past, he writes that "it is now invention itself that is a privilege".

At this late hour, the winter cold has invaded the room as Stanislas de Boufflers writes the last lines of his report. However, the Knight does not tremble. All he feels at that moment is the satisfaction of having accomplished his duty with seriousness and assiduity. Nonetheless, as a military veteran, he knows that it is too early to claim victory.

*

During the night of the 4th of August 1789, the abolition of all feudal privileges was passed, causing concern among inventors who had received privileges under the *Ancien Régime*. Privileges relating to inventions were apparently saved. However, the situation remained uncertain, and clarification was needed. This was why the National Assembly appointed the Knight of Boufflers, deputy of the nobility of the bailliage of Nancy, to compose a new law for the protection of inventions.

As it appears in the above story, the talent of a witty man was indeed necessary to achieve the synthesis between a policy that would encourage inventors of machines and industrial products (as indicated by the title of Boufflers' report) and erase any apparent connection with the privileges granted by the absolute monarchy, which had been disgraced. In other words, it was necessary to turn the page definitively without completely moving away from the past. The squaring of the circle was required.

Thanks to the rhetorical precautions and clever arguments of the Knight, the text of the law was adopted without debate on the 7th of January 1791. However, according to the law, the provisions would have to be supplemented by a decree of the Assembly. A second text was thus put to the vote. This one was fiercely opposed by some deputies, but they did not succeed in preventing its adoption. While the law of the 7th of January did refer to "*patentes*", the implementing regulation of the 25th of May 1791 used the expression "*brevets d'invention*" for the first time. This may have been an additional trick to increase distance from the old privileges. In any case, the expression was clearly well chosen since it is still used today in France.

The first patent ("*brevet d'invention*") was granted on the 27th of July 1791 to Louis François Ollivier for a process of manufacturing English black earth. As the Revolution had not yet completed its emancipation from the monarchy, this patent was issued by King Louis XVI, barely a year and a half before he was guillotined.

The new law of 1791 linked the protection of inventions to the notion of land ownership and found its justification in the natural right of inventors to their inventions.

According to this law, patents were issued for a fixed period of 5, 10 or 15 years, at the inventor's choice, against the payment of onerous fees. Protection was extended to all processes and manufactured articles. In return for the granting of a patent, the inventor had to describe their invention in a way that allowed a person skilled in the art to reproduce it. However, publication measures were still very limited.

Although it offered a shift away from them, the law did not completely get rid of the mercantile motives of the old privileges. Indeed, in an obvious attempt to limit the diffusion of knowledge abroad, the French patent could be invalidated if the inventor sought to obtain a patent on the same invention in another country. On the other hand, an inventor who introduced into French territory an invention that had been patented in another country was granted the same rights in France as a local inventor (without exceeding, however, the duration of the foreign patent). Finally, any invention had to be utilized in the French territory within two years of the patent being granted or risk being invalidated by a judge.

The most fundamental consequence of the recognition of the inventor's natural right was certainly the immediate challenge it posed to the preliminary examination of inventions. As we have seen, prior to the French Revolution, this examination had been carried out with zeal by an absolutist state that wanted to control everything. From the moment that the right to an invention was considered to result naturally from the creative act, no third party was legitimate to dispute its validity anymore – neither scholars, nor guilds, nor agents of the state. The market became the sole judge. In order to guarantee the natural right and to preserve its credibility, the state therefore took a back seat. Upon being granted patents through a simple registration process, French inventors found themselves in a situation similar to that of their British counterparts, with whom there were to compete more and more.

As is clear from the work of historian Gabriel Galvez-Behar, a long period of embarrassment began for the French administration. On the one hand, it was forced to indicate on each patent that "the Government, by granting a patent without preliminary examination, does not intend to guarantee in any way the priority, the merit, or the success of an invention". On the other hand, it could not help but assist inventors by informing them of the prior art it was aware of, thereby violating the principle of no examinations.

The Knight of Boufflers had thus created an ambiguous system, which would be both successful and increasingly dissatisfying. Still, by placing inventions under the protection of a natural right, he had locked the system against any possibility of fundamental reform. It then took half a century for a new conception to be developed.

Patent for a beer manufacturing process
filed by Louis Pasteur on the 28th of June 1871

The expression "without government guarantee"
("*sans garantie du gouvernement*") is clearly visible.

THE LAWS OF NATURE ARE NOT IMMUTABLE

THE LAW OF 1844

After the tornado of the Revolution and the belligerence of the First Empire, under which Napoleon's troops confronted the majority of Europe's armies, a new period of stability and relative calm favorable to economic development and technical progress finally began. This was an opportunity for France, whose industrial lag behind Great Britain in particular had lengthened. The need to compete with foreign countries became a major national concern, taking precedence over more abstract considerations such as the inventor's natural right to dispose of their inventions.

At the same time, the notion of property itself had evolved such that the trade-off imposed by the Knight of Boufflers was no longer tenable. Indeed, property was now considered an absolute right that was subjected to no limitations. By the middle of the 19th century, the exception to this rule enshrined in maximum terms for patents could no longer be tolerated due to the contradiction it posed. In order to prevent such a conceptual collapse – the effects of which would have extended far beyond the field of inventions –, the natural right of inventors was declared over.

A new law was therefore adopted in 1844. Without completely departing from the 1791 law, it replaced the notion of property attached to patents with the less ambitious notion of an exclusive right to exploitation. This change did not call into question the idea of a contract between inventors and society, but the parameters of the contract were modified. From this point on, the granting of a patent no longer represented the official recognition by society of the inventor's natural right on their invention, but instead granted a reward to the inventor in return for a service rendered to society.

Moral considerations thus faded into the background, giving way to a utilitarian logic. In a way, the justification of the patent was again close to that of old privileges, as both offered temporary exclusivity in exchange for the provision of a technique useful to society. Only the role of a king or a queen in the granting of this right (and the elements of arbitrariness and favoritism this entailed) remained disposed of along with the monarchic past.

This new reversal reintroduced a problem already encountered in the past: how can the utility of a service rendered to society by an inventor be measured by a simple patent registration system? The law of 1844 chose not to reintroduce the preliminary examination, which had been officially abolished in 1791. The weakening of the role of the administration was even reinforced by the addition of an explicit mention that patents were issued "without government guarantee" ("*sans garantie du gouvernement*"), expressed in the form of the acronym "S.G.D.G." The lack of examination actually provided certain benefits, including a reduced cost to the state and inventors alike.

Apart from the courts, which were responsible for making decisions in case of a dispute, it was therefore the inventors who bore the heavy burden of determining whether or not their inventions deserved patent protection. Nevertheless, the public authorities still remained on the sidelines and did not really give inventors the means to make informed decisions. Indeed, despite the progress in publication measures set forth by the 1844 law, access to third party patents remained limited and difficult until 1902 at the earliest. Under these conditions, conducting relevant prior art searches to determine whether or not an invention was already known was a real challenge.

Despite some notable changes or improvements (such as staggering costs over time through the introduction of annual fees, abolishing patents granted for imported inventions, ending the forfeiture of a French patent because of the application for a corresponding patent abroad, etc.), the law of 1844 did not put an end to the logical critique of patents. This was all the more true at the beginning of the second half of the 19th century, when a powerful abolitionist movement was sweeping through Europe and France.

With the help of professionals (namely patent attorneys and lawyers) who developed their mastery of patents, the institution was able to persist despite the failings of the state. Nevertheless, new reforms were decided at the very beginning of the 20th century.

A dedicated office, the National Office of Industrial Property, was created in 1901 before being replaced in 1951 by the National Institute of Industrial Property (INPI). The not-so-young French industrial property specialists will no doubt remember the old convent in the heart of the 8th arrondissement of Paris where the INPI was once located, as well as the dreaded "night mailbox" housed in its façade, where patent applications had to be slipped in after the offices had closed in order to benefit from the day's filing date (which was essential to guarantee the novelty of an invention against a same-day disclosure).

Beyond its basic mission to grant patents, the INPI has always sought to offer a useful public service, for example by integrating private actors in the performance of its tasks. Many French patent attorneys have had the opportunity – as I have had myself – to make free permanence at the INPI. Here one spends the whole day encountering all types of inventors, from the mad genius to the founder of a promising start-up, all of whom dream of changing the world and hope to find in the patent the means of achieving of their ambition. The INPI also works to raise society's awareness of challenges to industrial property and to inform companies about the importance of building an appropriate patent strategy.

It is impossible to end this short history of the patent in France without mentioning a more recent evolution. A law of 1968, which has been amended several times since then, brought many changes to the grant procedure. In particular, a documentary opinion (*"avis documentaire"*) on the novelty of inventions (in the form of a list of relevant prior art references) began to be established for all patent applications after having been tested in the field of drugs. This represented a significant change from the registration system then in force in the country. The documentary opinion was replaced by a full search report in 1990. Although the 1968 law introduced into French law the inventive step criterion (according to which an invention must not be obvious from the prior art), it was not yet a criterion used for agreeing or refusing to grant a patent. Since the 22nd of May 2020, however, the inventive step assessment has been fully taken integrated in the examination performed by the INPI. This substantial change, which aims to reinforce the robustness of French patents, puts an end to a two-century legal parenthesis and should deal a fatal blow to France's solid reputation as the country without examination *par excellence*.

In spite of its hesitations, France has marked the history of patents and inspired many other countries in the creation of their own system. However, while the Knight of Boufflers was using his creativity to make patents last in the long term, a distant country, still under construction, was arriving with a bang on the world scene and would soon bring patents into the modern age.

NEW WORLD, NEW PATENT

THE UNITED STATES OF AMERICA

The first U.S. patent, granted to Samuel Hopkins
on the 31ˢᵗ of July 1790

SILICON EXTRACTED FROM
A PIECE OF PARCHMENT

SILICON VALLEY, 21ST CENTURY

For many years now, Richard Hendricks has been dreaming of changing the world and putting his extraordinary lines of code at the service of millions of users. However, even though he is a computer genius, he is still a naive and clumsy boy who freaks out when he has to speak in front of an audience. In short, he does not really fit the image of a start-up leader in the Silicon Valley...

And yet, he is the founder of a software company called Pied Piper. In order to create it, Richard has recruited brothers-in-arms who, while being original thinkers, share the same passion as him and are prepared to sacrifice anything to make Pied Piper a success. He has even managed to surround himself with a few trustworthy people, such as Erlich Bachman, the megalomaniac incubator who hosts him, Ron LaFlamme, the young dilettante lawyer, and Monica, who works for a venture capitalist and has taken Richard under her wing.

The problem is that if you want to succeed here, it is not enough to develop the best algorithm, hire the best talents or have the best marketing. You have to find your place in a complex ecosystem that wants to generate revenue quickly. Above all, you have to beat competitors who are ready to use any means to win the race and get to the top.

Richard has suffered countless setbacks at the hands of the technology company Hooli and its merciless leader, Gavin Belson. Already, while working on a revolutionary data compression algorithm, Richard has been taken to court by Hooli on the grounds that his compression technique had been developed using Hooli's work tools at the time Richard was employed there. As a result, the intellectual property attached to this technique was the property of Hooli, meaning that Pied Piper could not theoretically continue to operate. Richard's only salvation came from the unexpected invalidation of his former employment contract by the judge, due to an unlawful non-compete clause.

More recently, Richard has moved on to a project of a completely different scale: the design of a new, totally decentralized Internet, where data exchanges would be made through a network of cell phones. But fate and intellectual property are against Pied Piper: Richard has discovered that his concept was in fact an invention already patented by... Gavin Belson! The patent is so broad that it leaves Richard no hope of getting around it. Richard's dream would have been shattered if Gavin Belson, touched by grace, had not strangely decided to donate his patent to him.

This surprising event shocks Richard. That his worst enemy would give him such an important asset is perplexing. What did Gavin have in mind when he decided to transfer ownership of his patent to Richard? What could be behind this generous gift? Even as he spins the questions in his head, like a compiler unwinding lines of computer code, Richard cannot find an answer.

But it does not matter in the end. With the basic patent for a decentralized Internet in his hands, Richard can now look to the future with optimism. The challenges ahead are huge, of course, but the major obstacle to Pied Piper's development has just disappeared forever.

*

The above story is a condensed version of a few passages from the American television show *Silicon Valley*, created by Mike Judge, John Altschuler and Dave Krinsky and broadcasted on HBO from 2014 to 2019. This terrific and humorous series takes us into the heart of the start-up reactor: Silicon Valley.

California's "Silicon Valley" (named for the basic material used in computer chips) is home to an impressive concentration of cutting-edge industries, talented entrepreneurs and prestigious universities. Although other centers of excellence exist elsewhere in the country, Silicon Valley is a symbol. It represents the American dream, the promise that any willing individual can succeed and change the world for the better.

It is not surprising, then, that this place of all possibilities has inspired a television series aimed at the general public. It is also interesting to note that intellectual property in general, and patents in particular, have a prominent place in the plot. This is no accident. Patents have become an indispensable tool for any entrepreneur wishing to add their contribution to our technological world. It is also the instrument through which genius can express itself and participate in the creation of a spiral of innovation. In the United States, this belief did not originate in Silicon Valley. Rather, it is rooted in the very origins of the state, in a small piece of parchment from 1787 that gave the newly independent nation a Constitution.

Before independence, the British influence in North America was very strong, particularly in the application of the common law. Letters patents were therefore not unknown to the first settlers. As early as the 17th century, exclusive rights were granted to inventors in the New World. The very first one was granted to Samuel Winslow in 1641 in the state of Massachusetts for a method of salt production. In fact, a strong desire to innovate appeared very early on in the thirteen American colonies, which may seem natural in a huge territory where everything had to be built and where newcomers had to show initiative to find their place and start a new life.

Eleven years after the proclamation of the United States Declaration of Independence in 1776, a convention was held in Philadelphia under the presidency of George Washington. This convention resulted in a draft Constitution, consisting of a short preamble followed by seven articles, which was ratified the following year. Its first article clearly expressed the country's will to promote the progress of science and useful arts by guaranteeing authors and inventors the exclusive right to their writings and discoveries, although for a limited term. This provision set in stone the principle of the American patent (and that of copyright).

Its placement in the first article (and the fact that it is the only place in the entire Constitution where the word "right" appears) show the importance that the drafters afforded the patent. Rather than providing for its mere possibility, the idea of "securing" an inventor's exclusive right to their invention further strengthens the commitment. This may sound surprising considering that the United States was then a fledgling country, poorly developed, essentially agrarian and ruined by the war of independence. It was very far, therefore, from being the world leader it would become more than a century later. In practice, this guarantee given to inventors amounted to granting them real property rights over their inventions.

This allowed the conclusion of licensing or assignment agreements and facilitated commercial transactions of all kinds. As a result, many inventors quickly joined forces with entrepreneurs (when they did not play this role themselves) to market their inventions.

This founding text reveals another enlightening element. It deliberately framed the exclusive right granted to inventors in a peculiar perspective, according to which the recognition of the inventor's inherent, quasi-sacred right to their work would guarantee the perpetuation of technical progress. The protection of inventors' interests would thus coincide perfectly with the needs of welfare and the economic development of society. This convergence of interests is at the core of the American utilitarian conception of the patent and of the dynamism that this concept has produced, from the Constitution to the actors – both fictional and real – of the Silicon Valley.

In the application of the Constitution, and in a timeframe close to that of revolutionary France, the first American law on patents was adopted in 1790. It was one of the first federal laws, binding all states.

The first patent issued under this new law dates from the 31st of July 1790. It was granted to Samuel Hopkins for a method of making potash and bore the signature of the first president, George Washington. In addition to being an inventor, Hopkins was an entrepreneur who made profit from his patent by licensing it to third parties.

The 1790 law, which took up some of the terms of the English Statute of Monopolies, reserved the granting of a patent only to the "first and true inventor". The latter had to submit an application including a "sufficient" description of their invention. Contrary to the English case, however, the "first and true inventor" principle was applied literally from the outset, since U.S. patents were granted only for inventions with absolute novelty (i.e. that had not already been invented, either in the United States or elsewhere in the world). According to the same logic, importers were not considered to be inventors. Another British-inspired characteristic also appeared: the U.S. patent was granted for a 14-year term.

In contrast to the situation in England and other European countries, the U.S. patent system was designed to be affordable. The fees charged were relatively modest and lower than those of other systems by a factor of roughly 10. The patent was thus accessible to all. This democratization of the patent contributed to the success of the American system. In this respect, it is interesting to note that although the patent was initially open only to American citizens – a limitation that was lifted in 1861 –, it was accessible to women from the outset. The first article of the law of 1790 put men and women on an equal footing: "he, she, or they, hath or have invented or discovered..."

One of the main characteristics of the 1790 law is that it provided that all patent applications be subject to an examination to verify their compliance with the law, as well as to check the novelty and utility of the invention to be protected. This examination was carried out by the "Patent Board", made up of three eminent personalities: the Secretary of State, at the time Thomas Jefferson, the Attorney General, Edmund Randolph, and the Minister of War, Henry Knox. This board issued a total of about 60 patents and rejected many others, which were deemed to be known or unworkable inventions.

Although the grant procedure was fairly simple, especially in comparison with the English procedure, the examination of patent applications quickly turned out to be inefficient. The three personalities mentioned above had little time to devote to this labor intensive task. The Patent Board usually met only on the last Saturday of each month.

To solve this problem, a reform of the law was introduced in 1793. The new text went against the law of 1790 by establishing a regime of simple registration with no prior examination. This meant that virtually all patent applications were accepted and that the courts had the burden of determining the validity of patents in the event of a dispute. This system was no more satisfactory than the previous one, and the need for a new reform was soon felt. However, the next reform would do a much better job and would truly lay the foundations of the modern patent.

The Herbert C. Hoover Building is still pictured on the front page
of each "U.S. priority document" printed by the U.S. Patent Office.

THE FIRE OF GENIUS

A WALK IN WASHINGTON D.C.

If you walk in Washington D.C., you may have the confused feeling of being in the very heart of the United States, because of its status as the capital and the large number of prestigious institutions that are located there. Paradoxically, however, it is also a place that is not like other American cities. The absence of skyscrapers, the width of the avenues, the sculpted façades and the many museums all around the city could make you think, at times, that you are in Paris. This is probably a nod to the French engineer and architect Pierre Charles L'Enfant, who initiated the construction of the city on the banks of the Potomac in 1791.

Let us start our walk in the colorful Chinatown area. We are near the large Friendship Archway that celebrates the affinity between Washington and Beijing. As we walk down 7th Street NW to the intersection of G Street, we come upon a splendid building that houses the Smithsonian American Art Museum and the National Portrait Gallery. The neoclassical style building, which covers an entire block, is impressive.

Its construction began in 1836 to house the Patent Office, the authority responsible for granting patents to inventors. The Blodgett's Hotel, where the predecessor of this institution sat, had indeed burned down that year (the patents granted began to be numbered by the office following this unfortunate event). The imposing size of the building is partly explained by the fact that, for each patent application, a working model of the invention had to be stored there. In 1877, this building was also destroyed by fire and tens of thousands of models and archives went up in smoke. It was then restored and its activity continued until 1932. Its destruction was barely avoided in the early 1950s.

Let us continue our stroll in space and time, towards the White House, further west. After passing the Ford's Theatre, where President Lincoln was assassinated, and the Warner Theatre, we reach Pennsylvania Avenue, where we pass the office of the Mayor of the city. Just before reaching 15th Street, which borders the President's Park, we stop in front of the monumental Herbert C. Hoover Building, which currently houses the Department of Commerce as well as the White House Visitor Center. Its location in the famous "Federal Triangle" and its dimensions are quite exceptional. When it was completed in 1932, it was the tallest building in the world!

For more than 30 years after its construction, the Hoover Building housed the Patent Office and its largest room was used as a public space to allow inventors and their representatives to search through the millions of patents stored there. The building façade is well known to patent professionals around the world, as it is pictured on the front page of every "U.S. priority document" (certifying the number and date of the first patent filed on an invention in the United States).

As we approach the 15th Street entrance of the Hoover Building, we can see the following inscription engraved on its pediment: "The patent system added the fuel of interest to the fire *of genius". This quote is taken from an 1858 speech by Abraham Lincoln. Lincoln was not yet president of the United States, but he was already an inventor and the holder of patent No. 6.469, issued in 1849, for buoying vessels over shoals. The quote echoes the majesty of the building. It perfectly sums up the American conception of patents, which managed to institute an incentive framework enabling the genius that resides in each individual to express its full creative potential. The Patent Office certainly deserved the architectural jewels that Washington had to offer since, in the permanent race of the United States towards progress, it would play a fundamental role.*

*

The construction of the first building we came across on our walk in Washington coincided with the creation of the modern Patent Office, provided for by a new law of 1836. This law marked a real turning point. Firstly, because the office was conceived as an administrative institution headed by a commissioner, assisted by a clerk and a few specialized agents, whose activity was dedicated to granting patents. Secondly, because, in a shift away from the unsatisfactory registration procedure introduced in 1793, the new law entrusted the Patent Office with the task of carrying out the objective examination of patent applications, focusing on the novelty and utility of inventions. The option to appeal in case of rejection was also provided. This modern examination of patentability requirements by qualified staff was a world first that many other countries would adopt decades later.

To better define the scope of inventions and to facilitate their examination by the Patent Office, the 1836 law also introduced a major legal innovation: the "claims". These constituted the refined expression of what the inventor truly considered to be their invention over which they would claim an exclusive right. They did not replace the detailed description of the invention, which may have contained one or more specific embodiments, but they supplemented it to precisely outline the scope of the protection sought. Those who have already had to draft claims know how difficult the exercise is because of its formalism and the high level of abstraction it requires. The claims make up the basic element of a patent, from which the office assesses the patentability requirements and the courts decide on infringement (i.e. the reproduction of the patented invention by unauthorized third parties). Overly broad claims capturing part of the prior art will normally be rejected for lack of novelty, while overly narrow claims are likely to render patent protection ineffective or useless. It is therefore understandable why inventors often entrust the drafting of their patents to specialized attorneys, whose expertise is one of the keys to success. The introduction of claims by the law of 1836 is all the more remarkable since other countries did not introduce claims until much later (1883 in England and 1968 in France, for example).

In matters of law, as in technology, innovation can snowball. The legal and institutional framework created by the law of 1836 paved the way for an avalanche of other innovations that would mark the following decades. The judicial system played an important role in the development of the rules, applying the founding principles of the Constitution in such a way as to maintain a balance between securing the exclusive rights of inventors (there were virtually no limitations on the rights of patent holders at the time, unlike the situation in other countries) and preserving the interests of society as a whole.

One example of a legal innovation introduced by the American courts in the 19th century is the creation of the concept of "non-obviousness" as a criterion for patentability. As we have seen, in order to be patentable, an invention must be new – i.e. different from what was previously known. However, what happens when the novelty of an invention is based on a minor deviation from the prior art? Granting a patent on such an invention would incur an excessive social cost by creating exclusivity around an object that was totally within the reach of the "skilled person" (a hypothetical character with usual technical knowledge in the field of the invention). The American Patent Act of 1793, taking up almost word for word a provision of the French patent law of 1791, provided that an invention could not concern a simple change to the form or the proportions of any machine or composition. The 1836 Act removed this proviso, so the Supreme Court had to step in and try to clarify. It did so in 1851 in the *Hotchkiss v. Greenwood* ruling, a case involving doorknobs made of terra cotta or porcelain, rather than wood or metal as was standard at the time. The Supreme Court ruled that, in order to be patentable, an invention had to be the product of more ingenuity and skill than possessed by an ordinary person skilled in the art. This judgment marked a clear desire to prevent the protection of inventions that were not very inventive, but the vagueness of the criterion used was interpreted differently by the courts. The issue was finally settled a century later when the 1952 Patent Act added the U.S.C. Section § 103, which codified the criterion of non-obviousness that we use today: an invention cannot be patented if it would have been obvious to a person having ordinary skill in the art at the time it was made.

Other innovations in the law that emerged in the United States in the 19th century include: the gradual strengthening of publication measures, so as to improve the dissemination of knowledge; the extension, in 1861, of the patent protection term from 14 to 17 years from the date of its granting (the current term of 20 years from filing would not be adopted until 1995); and the creation, in 1859, of immunity from loss of novelty of an invention disclosed as a result of its patent protection abroad, foreshadowing the future "priority right" that will be discussed further below.

These numerous advances demonstrate the vitality of the American patent system at a time when national industry was booming. In fact, the number of patents filed annually exceeded that of France in 1865. Some believe that the patent system is part of the reason for the country's irresistible economic development. This was the case made by Takahashi Korekiyo, a future Japanese minister, who visited the United States in 1886 and was so impressed by the country's patent system that he recommended that it be transposed to Japan upon his return.

The dynamism of U.S. patents did not wane during or since the 20th century. Businesses have progressively taken control of the tool, using it in increasingly strategic ways. As for universities, research centers and non-profit organizations benefiting from public funds, the Bayh-Dole Act allowed them to obtain patents on their inventions starting in 1980.

In 1982, the creation of the Court of Appeals for the Federal Circuit (CAFC) as a second-instance court with exclusive jurisdiction over patents nationwide has led to greater uniformity in case law and has overall strengthened the rights of patent owners.

The most recent major reform in U.S. history came in 2011. Known as the *America Invents Act* (AIA), it introduced numerous changes to U.S. patent practice. The most significant change concerned the fundamental question of who owns the right to a patent. Previously, the right to a patent belonged to the first inventor ("*first to invent*"). Since 2013, as a result of the AIA, the right to a patent now belongs to the first applicant ("*first to file*"), or more precisely – to remain consistent with the founding principles of the Constitution – to the first inventor to file. This important change marked an alignment of the United States with the system applicable in the rest of the world.

The above story took us through the streets of Washington. Since the late 1960s, however, the Patent

Office is no longer based in the capital. After a stint in Crystal City, Virginia (where it became the *Patent and Trademark Office*), it moved to Alexandria where it has remained since 2005. The splendor of the old Washington buildings reminds us of the importance of this institution in the history of a democracy with an exceptional destiny. Likewise, while numerous amendments have been made spanning nearly two centuries, the 1836 Act still largely imbues the current U.S. patent system.

Despite the dazzling success of the United States, it would be wrong to believe that the patent is the object of absolute consensus there. Even in a country where dreams and reality sometimes blur together, opinions confront each other and doubt is allowed...

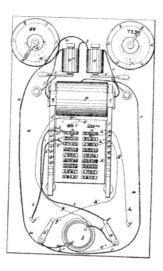

T. A. EDISON.

Electric Vote-Recorder.

No. 90,646.

Patented June 1, 1869.

Witnesses.

Inventor

The first patent of Thomas Edison,
granted in 1869 under number U.S. 0,090,646

It covers a voting machine that was not successful.

Source: Espacenet - Public domain

EVEN IN THE LAND OF DREAMS, DOUBT IS ALLOWED

The United States has provided us with some of the best examples of "success stories" featuring inventors as protagonists.

How could one not admire the career of Samuel Morse (1791-1872), an American painter who was never destined to become an inventor? Yet he made remarkable advances in the development of the electric telegraph and the binary code of dots and dashes that was named after him. This technology led to the first transatlantic communication by submarine cable in 1858. For his inventions, Morse filed patents that allowed him to delegate marketing to trusted third parties.

And what about Thomas Edison (1847-1931), a prolific inventor with more than 1,000 patents to his name, creator of research laboratories and co-founder of General Electric? Or the Serbian Nikola Tesla (1856-1943), who emigrated to the United States before the age of 30 to work with Edison? Tesla was one of the most creative inventors of his time, particularly in the fields of electricity and electromagnetism, with some 300 patents to his credit. Or Graham Bell (1847-1922), who became a naturalized American in 1882 and co-founded the company AT&T after obtaining a patent on the telephone in 1876 (even though it is known now that Elisha Gray had patented the same invention two hours before Bell and that the Italian-American Antonio Meucci had created a similar device a few years earlier)?

These and many other exceptional characters have made the United States the technology leader it is today. Patents were essential to each of their success, providing third-party financing, partnerships with talented businessmen, and public admiration. It is hard to imagine what the world would be like today without the brilliant inventions of these figures – or the patents that helped turn them into innovations that everyone could use.

These remarkable achievements might lead some to believe that the patent is uncriticised and uncontested in the United States. The reality is much more nuanced. Even if the patent has had a prominent place in the history of the country from the outset, reservations were expressed about it very early on. Admittedly, the United States was built in part in opposition to the idea of monopoly, notably the one granted in 1773 by the British Parliament to the British East India Company over the sale of tea in the American colonies. This monopoly on tea set off the Boston Tea Party revolt, a prelude to the Revolutionary War. It is therefore easy to understand why the Constitution deliberately avoided the confiscatory notion of monopoly, preferring instead to frame the patent as a form of exclusive right.

One of the authors of the Declaration of Independence and the U.S. Constitution was the famous Benjamin Franklin. This man was a polymath. Before entering politics, he was not only a printer, journalist, editor and philosopher, but also a physicist and inventor! We owe to him the invention of the lightning rod. However, Franklin never sought to obtain exclusive rights to his inventions. As he stated in his autobiography, he considered creative activity to be a useful service that should be given to society with generosity.

Even more surprisingly, Thomas Jefferson himself, despite being one of the three members of the Patent Board, was reserved about the scope of the patent right. In a reply written to a man named Isaac McPherson in 1813, Jefferson gave us valuable insight into his thinking. He stated, in contrast to the French approach of the time, that inventors had no natural right to their inventions. According to him, like a candle that does not lose its luster when it lights another, ideas should be allowed to disseminate freely without alteration. Nevertheless, Jefferson believed that society could legitimately decide, for its own benefit, to grant an exclusive right on the fruits of inventions, in order to encourage the generation of further useful ideas. This was the utilitarian view expressed in the Constitution of 1787 (although Jefferson, then working as an ambassador in France, did not participate in its drafting).

Jefferson's position on the Patent Board actually allowed him to establish rules to prevent the "embarrassment" caused by an exclusive patent from outweighing the benefits of the invention to society. One of these rules stated that an invention could not be patented if it consisted of a mere change in application, material or form. Rather than showing a preconceived hostility to patents, Jefferson was concerned with avoiding excessive monopolies and establishing balance in the application of the law.

Some consider that Jefferson's position reflects a more general opposition among the founding fathers of the American nation to the concept of intellectual property. This thesis does not fit well, however, with the content of Article I of the Constitution. Like 18th century England, it seems that the early United States was in fact more receptive to the theory of the natural rights of inventors than Jefferson's writings suggest.

Subsequently, the patent enjoyed varying degrees of support in American society at different times. Towards the middle of the 19th century, in a context of developing liberalism, patents came under attack from committed opponents. Hostility spread to some American judges. The most daring proclaimed that the only valid patents were those that had not yet passed through their hands! Nonetheless, the system eventually overcame this crisis.

However, distrust of monopolies did not disappear, and while monopoly abuses existed in other contexts (agreements on prices and quantities produced, division of territories between competitors, etc.), patents were not immune to abusive behavior, which was regularly sanctioned by the courts. To fight effectively against these phenomena, the United States adopted anti-trust laws very early on. The first law, the Sherman Act, dates from 1890. Without this legal framework, would patent abuses have developed and led to increased criticism, to the point of questioning the merits of the patent?

In any event, U.S. law and case law have adapted over time, keeping pace with changes in public attitudes toward patents. In a pendulum swing, they have sometimes strengthened the rights given to patentees, like between the 1980s and 2000s, and sometimes weakened them, like the period since the mid-2000s. In recent years, court decisions have, for example, considerably reduced the ability of patentees to obtain injunctive relief to cease infringing activities, expanded the possibilities for third parties to challenge the validity of patents, and blurred the ability of inventions to meet the patentability requirements in the fields of biotechnology or software. Some voices are now speaking out against what they see as the excessive weakening of U.S. patent law. Others even denounce the American system as "broken", which would threaten the country's capacity for innovation.

In short, the debate over the scope of the patent right is far from over, and opposing views can be expected to continue to confront each other as the patent continues to reinvent itself.

But while the patent has certainly not been without its critics in the United States, it is in the heart of Europe that the attack on it has been strongest. So strong, in fact, that it could have won...

TO EACH THEIR OWN PATH

THE LAST BASTIONS OF RESISTANCE

THE NETHERLANDS; SWITZERLAND

OCTROOIRAAD NEDERLAND.

BIBLIOTHEEK
No.
BUREAU VOOR DEN
INDUSTRIEELEN EIGENDOM

OCTROOI

No. 1.

KLASSE 12 p.

Aanvrage No. 514 Ned. ingediend . : 21 Juni 1912 te 12 uur 50 minuten n.m.
Aanvrage openbaargemaakt . . : 16 September 1912.
Octrooischrift uitgegeven . . . . . . : 7 Mei 1913.
Dagteekening van het octrooi . . : 3 April 1913.
Voorrang overeenkomstig art. 7 der
Octrooiwet 1910, Stbl. No. 313, vanaf : 4 Juli 1911 (Duitschland).

C. F. BOEHRINGER & ZONEN,

Fabriek van Chemische producten, te Mannheim-Waldhof (Duitschland).

Werkwijze ter bereiding van dubbelzouten van morphine en narkotine voor therapeutisch gebruik.

Bij de toepassing van morphine in de geneeskunde is de verlamming van het ademhalingscentrum, in vele gevallen, als ongewenschte nevenwerking waar te nemen.

Nu werd het tot heden onbekende feit ontdekt, dat deze nevenwerking belangrijk verminderd en zelfs geheel onderdrukt kan worden, wanneer men, tegelijk met de morphine, zekere hoeveelheid narkotine toedient. Voor dit doel was het natuurlijk gewenscht in de praktijk over eenvoudige verbindingen te beschikken, in welke de beide alkaloïden in eens constante verhouding aanwezig zijn, en de vervaardiging van zulke verbindingen is — zooals de desbetreffende proeven hebben uitgewezen — inderdaad mogelijk, wanneer men twee- en meerbasische zuren op morphine en narkotine laat inwerken en wel zoo, dat de ontstaande zouten de beide alkaloïden in dezelfde moleculaire verhouding of in de verhouding van 1 molecule morphine en twee en meer moleculen narkotine of van 1 molecule narkotine op twee en meer moleculen morphine bevatten. De vervaardiging der nieuwe verbindingen kan op verschillende manieren geschieden, bijv. door indamping der waterige of alkoholische oplossing der samenstellende deelen, door neerslaan van hare alkoholische oplossing

met aether of door dubbele omzetting harer zouten.

De nieuwe verbindingen zijn kristallijne stoffen, die veelal in alkohol gemakkelijk oplossen en ook in warm water goed oplosbaar zijn; in koud water loossen vele van haar evenens vrij goed op; in aether en andere gebruikelijke organische oplossingsmiddelen zijn zij echter onoplosbaar. Bijzonder geschikt voor geneeskundige toepassing is gebleken het zout, bestaande uit 1 molecule morphine en 1 molecule narkotine met 1 molecule mekonzuur, het zaur, dat ook in de opium in verbinding met de genoemde alkaloïden wordt aangetroffen.

Voorbeelden.

1) *Mekonzuur — Morphine — Narkotine.*

$C_7H_4O_7.C_{17}H_{19}NO_3.C_{22}H_{24}NO_7+4H_2O.$

2,54 deelen mekonzuur worden in ongeveer 50 deelen alkohol onder verwarming opgelost en achtereenvolgens 3,03 deelen fijne poedervormige morphine en 4,13 deelen narkotine bijgevoegd.

De gefiltreerde oplossing wordt met aether neergeslagen, waardoor men het zout in homogene witte kristalletjes verkrijgt, die

---

The first Dutch patent filed under the new regime
on the 21st of June 1912

Source: Espacenet - Public domain

A NEAR-FATAL ATTACK

ABOLITION OF THE DUTCH PATENT LAW, 1869

"The floor is open to the opposition!". The announcement resounds in the House of Representatives and restores, for a few seconds, the semblance of calm and serenity.

That the patent law in force in the Netherlands since 1817 is obsolete and inadequate is not a matter of doubt for any of the parliamentarians taking part in the debates on that day of 1869. After all, this law represents a mere continuation of the old practice of royal privileges. Moreover, the scope of patents has been reduced to a trickle by the restrictive interpretation of the courts. Still, the parliamentarians are in a fierce battle over what to do about the 1817 law, and now the majority has just argued for its outright abolition. Even though the issue has been debated in the country for many years, this time the Van Bosse-Fock government seems determined to make a radical decision.

Jan Heemskerk Abrahamszoon knows that the future of the patent depends in part on him. He is the one to whom all eyes now turn to counter the government's arguments in favor of abolition. Heemskerk is a well-informed jurist and knows the issue inside out. A few months earlier, while serving as Minister of the Interior in the previous government, the former liberal had converted to conservatism and taken a position in favor of a meager reform of the law as Belgium had done in 1854. As an experienced politician, he knows that his arguments will be difficult to develop today. But he is not a man to give up in the face of adversity.

Heemskerk slowly stands up and, after taking a long breath, speaks to the assembly on behalf of the opposition:

> *"Gentlemen, the government has told us that patents only make sense if there is a natural right of the inventors to their inventions, that is, a property right. But, according to the government, the temporary nature of the patent would be incompatible with the concept of property. In fact, the state could very well adopt a more flexible definition of property, which would no longer require an indefinite duration. Moreover, Roman law taught us that he who takes possession of a thing becomes his owner and that no one can enrich himself at the expense of others. It follows from these teachings that the inventor must be the owner of his own inventions and that no one should be able to copy them at the risk of enriching himself at the expense of the inventor."*

Heemskerk pauses to look into the eyes of his opponents. He knows that, if he is not followed on the strong argument of the natural right, his task will be much more complicated. Before he can even assess the effect of his introduction, Heemskerk is met with a murmur of disapproval. Among the snatches of sentences he picks up, he hears that property would only be applicable to tangible objects, not to inventions, and that monopolies from a bygone era should be done away with once and for all. Heemskerk then decides to continue on another level, that of the utility of patents:

"Gentlemen, please... Let us go further. The government bases its request for the abolition of our patent system on the idea that it satisfies neither the real interests of our industries nor the public interest of our society. To support this claim, the government has tried to make us believe that patents are a source of legal disputes. As far as I am concerned, I have counted only two patent disputes since 1817!"

Heemskerk pauses for a moment, sure that his argument has hit the mark. He sees with satisfaction a glint of embarrassment in the eyes of the majority members. He then continues:

"Do you have any idea of how much work, time and capital it takes to make an invention? Do you really think that inventors would be willing to make such sacrifices without the incentive of a patent? No, gentlemen, without patents, our inventors would keep their best techniques for themselves under secrecy, thus depriving other potential inventors of know-how that is indispensable to their own developments..."

Catching his breath, Heemskerk continues, straining his voice to drown out the noise:

"As for the case of Switzerland, which the government has put forward, I would like to point out to this Honourable House that the Netherlands is not Switzerland! It is true that Switzerland is quite successful without having a patent system in place. But do not forget that it has a more developed domestic industry than we do. Moreover, Swiss inventors regularly apply for patents abroad. Their independence from patents is therefore quite relative! As far as I am concerned, I prefer not to live in a country that bases its economic development, in an unfair and immoral way, on the imitation of inventions made elsewhere!"

111

At this point, the reactions to Heemskerk's words become louder. The murmurs turn into invective. The value judgement on their country suggested by the former minister shocks some parliamentarians who can no longer stand still.

Heemskerk understands that his time to speak is now limited. So, seeking to make a mark, he tries to undermine the confidence of the abolitionists by pronouncing a final warning:

> *"Dear colleagues, I understand your desire to turn the page on a flawed law. I know that some of you want our country to be part of the powerful anti-patent movement that has emerged around the world. Perhaps our government even imagines that the Netherlands should lead the way in abolition, taking other countries with it. This is a dangerous gamble. Radicality is rarely a vehicle for progress. Therefore, I conclude by calling on this assembly to be responsible: reform the law of 1817, rather than abolish it!"*

As he returns to his seat, Heemskerk feels a strange fatigue that he is not used to. He has done his best to defend a patent system that he feels is fair and useful, but the hostility he has perceived in the House gives him little hope about the outcome of the votes.

A wry smile then appears on his lips. Heemskerk's political career is far from over, and he now wonders whether he may ever himself have to lead a country without patents.

*

In the Netherlands, like elsewhere in Europe, inventions had been protected since the 16th century by means of royal privileges. However, the occupation of the country by France at the turn of the 18th century introduced new ideas inspired by the French Revolution. When the country was annexed in 1810, the French patent laws of 1791 were imposed. After independence was regained, the Netherlands adopted a national patent law in 1817. This law, which distanced itself from the French regime of property for inventors, suffered from several flaws that brought it closer to the old privileges with their arbitrary nature. In the middle of the 19th century, awareness of the imperfections of the 1817 law led to a growing distrust of the system and pushed successive Dutch governments to work on an alternative solution. The need for change became more pressing when, in 1854, Belgium, which had previously shared a common regime with the Netherlands, adopted its own patent law.

The above story relates to the final phase of a 13-year process during which various governments of the Netherlands hesitated about which regime to establish in the country in place of the 1817 law. Finally, it was the liberal Van Bosse-Fock government, which had just taken office, that took the bold step of proposing the abolition of the law, rather than its reform. The parliamentary debate described above took place in 1869. The discussed bill provided that no more new patents would be issued while allowing the renewal of already issued patents. While the form of the debate told above includes an element of imagination, the various arguments put forward by the former minister Heemskerk in response to those of the government are faithful to reality. This faithfulness to the facts was made possible by the valuable research work published by Professor Stef van Gompel.

Nowadays, the Van Bosse-Fock government's proposal to abolish patents overnight may seem courageous or risky, depending on one's point of view. This is especially true since no country had dared to take such an initiative before. However, the audacity it required must be put into perspective in view of the hostility to patents that spread throughout most of the developed world in the late 1860s.

As suggested in the above account, the government must have sincerely believed that the abolition of patents was a progressive step (like the abolition of the death penalty, also introduced by the same government the following year), which would be copied by other countries in its wake.

Economic liberalism was indeed the current of thought in vogue at the time. While very present in Great Britain, the land of Adam Smith and David Ricardo, it spread like wildfire through Europe in the middle of the 19th century. This movement had two focal points: the promotion of free trade, which led, for example, to the free trade treaties of Napoleon III's France with Great Britain in 1860 and with the German customs union, the Zollverein, in 1862; and the fight against monopolies, with which patents were assimilated. On this second front, the image of patents deteriorated so much that calls for their abolition increased. In 1869, the year of the vote on abolition in the Netherlands, the liberal British newspaper *The Economist* even predicted that the end of patents was near!

In this context, it is easy to understand the Dutch government's desire to put an end to a system that was so despised. This is all the more justified since the Netherlands had an economy that was much more oriented towards trade than towards industry at the time. Almost 90% of Dutch patents were granted to foreign applicants. Cancelling patent rights in the country would therefore amount to allowing a local industry to develop through the uncompensated use of technologies developed abroad. Rather than the patent itself, it was therefore its unsuitability to the national economy of the time that the Netherlands sought to eliminate with its abolition project.

Despite the criticism of some members of parliament, including Heemskerk, the abolition of patents was finally passed by an overwhelming majority (49 votes against 8 in the House of Representatives and 29 against 1 in the Senate), making the Netherlands the first and, to this day, only country in the world to have taken such a drastic measure against patents. Hence, Heemskerk, who later had important political responsibilities such as heading the government, indeed had to lead a patent-free country!

Like in the story above, the Dutch and Swiss situations are often compared. Indeed, the liberal controversy led Switzerland to postpone the adoption of a patent system several times as the Netherlands was getting rid of theirs. The comparison should not be taken too far, however. In contrast to the Netherlands, Switzerland in the second half of the 19th century was an innovative country. Its innovation was however limited to a few artisanal sectors, such as watchmaking and chocolate, where protection by secrecy could be sufficient, at least initially. Moreover, the modest size of the country and its limited domestic market did not encourage inventors to incur large expenses for the protection of their inventions. In industrial sectors suitable for export, rather than a local protection, Swiss inventors sought to obtain foreign patents directly in the promising markets they were targeting. These are reasons that may explain the Swiss lack of enthusiasm towards creating a national patent system.

Nevertheless, Switzerland finally adopted a patent law in 1888, which was then strengthened in 1907. As for the Netherlands, it re-established its patent system in 1912. If it seems they both finally aligned, it is partly because of a certain international pressure, but also because the cost/benefit ratio of patents had decreased for both over time. For example, mass production and the growing competitiveness of the United States in key traditional Swiss sectors made Switzerland fear falling behind, even in its own market. The patent then appeared as a way to slow down this movement and regain control.

Another reason for the reversal of these last bastions of resistance was the rapid and unexpected exhaustion of the liberal wave in the early 1870s. At that time, a deep economic crisis broke out in Europe, which liberalism was able to neither avoid nor contain. Finding markets for the industry products became a priority in each country. This required returning to protectionism on the domestic front. On the outside, free trade gave way to the conquest of new markets. The patent, which had been the object of criticism for several years, suddenly appeared as a means of supporting these new strategies to overcome the crisis. This marked the end of the strongest anti-patent movement in history.

No matter what one thinks of this outcome, the unique experience of the Netherlands and Switzerland is a noteworthy and instructive episode, as will be discussed later. Moreover, it is clear that the patent has shown remarkable resilience. Given that the patent was considered part of the problem during the years of opposition, one would be understandably surprised by its strange capacity to present itself, once the storm has passed, as part of the solution.

One thing remains certain: if the patent has been able to re-invent itself over time, the changes it has undergone since the 19th century no longer come from just a handful of nations. A growing number of countries have made their own original contributions to the construction and improvement of a system that is becoming more and more important.

LEGAL INNOVATION ON ALL FRONTS

The first German patent, granted to Johannes Zeltner
on the 2nd of July 1877.

From mistrust to excellence

Germany

According to figures released by national patent offices, the number of new patent applications filed in 2019 was 67,432 in Germany, compared to 19,250 in the UK and 15,812 in France. German national filings were therefore between 3.5 and 4.5 times greater than their European counterparts. If we look at the origin of European patent applications filed with the European Patent Office, we find a similar proportion (25,954 filings of German origin, compared to 10,554 of French origin and 5,715 of British origin in 2020). The proportion of patent disputes before national courts is also heavily in favor of Germany (and not just because distinct courts try infringement and validity issues separately in that country, whereas French and British courts consider and rule on both simultaneously).

In short, whatever the metric used, Germany's current supremacy in the European realm of patents is doubtless. This dominance radiates beyond Europe, as the German patent office was the sixth largest in the world in terms of patent filings in 2019, according to global statistics published by WIPO. The attractiveness of the German system continues (certainly helped by the presence of the

European Patent Office headquarters in Munich), and the excellence of German IP professionals is recognized far beyond the country's borders.

In view of this reality, it is hard to believe that the German patent system is a relatively recent construction and that the country's attitude towards patents has not always been kind.

In the 16th century, what would later become the German nation was still a multitude of juxtaposed states. These states were much more agricultural than industrial, and at first granted very few royal privileges for inventions. Things began to change at the end of the century, when the -power of Prussia came to establish itself. The first turning point came in the 17th century with the reign of Frederick II the Great, who brought Prussia into the circle of European powers through strong economic and territorial developments. The granting of arbitrary privileges increased, despite a certain unpopularity.

A new change occurred in 1815 when Prussia adopted legislation that provided a legal framework for patents and made their granting subject to strict conditions. In particular, an examination by experts was a prerequisite for any grant. Only a small proportion of the applications examined resulted in granted patents, and for the rare patents that successfully passed the examination, the protection they conferred to their holders remained limited. For example, their variable term did not exceed 3 years on average. Mistrust was the order of the day.

Then came the liberal wave mentioned above. It hit Prussia with particular acuity. It must be said that Chancellor Bismarck himself was very hostile to patents. He even went so far as to advocate the abolition of patents rather than their reform in 1868. Without the effective backing of its supporters (industry and practitioners), the patent might have met the same fate in Prussia as it did in the Netherlands.

In the course of the 19th century, other German states adopted their own patent policies, which led to a great disparity. Following the Franco-Prussian war of 1870, Alsace-Lorraine adopted a system close to that of France, while other states, such as Hamburg, simply did not offer any patent protection.

The most significant development occurred after the creation of the German Empire in 1871, which unified the various states within a single entity. A national patent law was indeed created in 1877. The fact that it came late in comparison with other industrial powers was in fact an advantage, because German law could draw inspiration from foreign systems and sought to retain the best aspects of each. In this respect, the influence of the American system was particularly strong.

Thus, the law of 1877 established a central administration in charge of granting German patents: the *Kaiserliches Patentamt*, located in Berlin. According to this law, the right to a patent belongs to the first applicant (first-to-file system), whether or not they are the first and true inventor. This was an important simplification which saved the administration from having to search for the origin and the real circumstances surrounding the conception of an invention. For industrial companies, which had then become one of the main sources of innovation, the first-to-file system also guaranteed legal security against attempts by third parties to claim paternity of patented inventions *a posteriori*.

Forty years after the United States, Germany became the second country to introduce a grant procedure including a systematic examination of patent applications by technical experts. These experts remained professionally active in their technical field and only performed their work as examiners as a complement. The German examination was severe, so that the patents actually granted were few in number but robust, and probably covered more innovative inventions than in other countries. This is due to the fact that the *Patentamt* conducted a thorough prior art search among German patents, some foreign patents, and across a diverse technical literature. In the same vein, case law then developed the notion of "inventive height" (*Erfindungshöhe*) – which was close to the American "non-obviousness" and would be replaced later by the concept of "inventive step" – to better exclude from patentability too minor variations of known techniques.

Patent applications began to be published even before being granted so that third parties could oppose them. This measure also contributed to the dissemination of knowledge and techniques, with the objective, on the part of the public authorities, of promoting economic development.

The term of protection was initially 15 years, before being extended to 18 years in 1923.

The first German patent was issued on the 2nd of July 1877, only one day after the opening of the *Patentamt*. It was granted to an inventor named Johannes Zeltner for a method of producing an ultramarine red pigment.

In addition to the German patent itself, another title was also created in Germany in 1871: the *Gebrauchmuster*. This utility model was a sort of "petty patent" – a simplified version, obtained without examination that granted a weaker protection than its big brother. Far from replacing the patent, the utility model offered inventors and their beneficiaries advantages that were complementary and cumulative with those of the patent.

After having itself learned from the foreign patent systems that preceded it, the German system would in turn become a source of inspiration for many other countries, notably in Northern Europe and as far away as Japan.

The first Japanese patent, granted to Zuisho Hotta
on the 14th of August 1885

AND ELSEWHERE?

What about elsewhere in the world? Industrial development and technical progress do not stop at borders. Genius exists wherever people live, especially when they are free. Patents are therefore not reserved for dominant economies. Many countries set up their own systems, inspired by what the precursor countries had developed before them while taking into account their particular needs.

The adoption of national patent laws was an opportunity to make various improvements aimed at making the system more efficient and more balanced. Some of these improvements, which were initially applied locally, would later become quasi-standards on a global scale. It can thus be said that the patents we know today have inherited the complex work of reflection, definition and enrichment involving many countries.

For example, Austria seems to be the first country to have introduced in 1832 a patent maintenance system paid for by periodic fees, the amount of which increases gradually. Thanks to this system, the cost of the patent remains relatively low during its first years, when the ability of the invention to become a successful innovation is still uncertain. The maintenance fees become much higher later on at a time when the patent holder is in a better position to assess the value of their title and the chances of success of their invention. In this way, the patent is financially accessible to a greatest number of people and the administration can be financed mainly by those that are kept for a long time and generate the most income. Moreover, the principle of fees that are paid gradually over time encourages patent holders to quickly abandon patents that cover the least promising inventions, thus allowing for their exploitation by third parties at an early stage. Despite variations between countries (e.g. annual or multi-year fee periods), the system of periodic and gradual maintenance fees has progressively become the norm.

The same Austrian law of 1832 also seems to be the first to have made it compulsory and systematic for patents to be available to the public by means of a dedicated publication.

However, let us leave Austria and take a look at Belgium. As mentioned above, Belgium adopted a patent law in 1854 under the watchful eye of the Netherlands. This Belgian law was the first to set the maximum term of patent protection to 20 years. As we saw earlier, the patent term varied considerably from one country to another and from one age to another. Some countries, such as France, had even given the inventor the choice between several possible terms. The 20-year term of protection selected by Belgium is universally recognized today.

What about more distant countries? It is clear that patents are not an exclusive prerogative of the Western world. Some Asian countries also became interested in them relatively early.

By the end of the 19th century, Japan was one of the new industrial powers. An experimental patent system briefly existed in the country in the early 1870s, then a first substantial patent law was passed in 1885. The first patent issued under this law was granted on the 14th of August 1885 to a man named Hotta Zuisho for an anti-corrosive lacquer to be applied to ship hulls. Following his previously outlined trip in 1886, the Japanese politician Takahashi Korekiyo recommended that Japan take inspiration from the patents of some of the countries he had visited, especially those of the United States. A new law put this recommendation into effect in 1888.

China is an ancient civilization. Its five millennia of existence have brought to the world an original contribution, rich in numerous inventions. In the long history of this country, the appearance of the patent is relatively recent (even if some forms of privileges seem to be attested to in ancient China). It was following the first opium war in 1840 that the modern patent entered the country. The colonial powers pushed the then ruling Qing dynasty to adopt a patent system based on the Western model. As a result, the first Chinese patent law was passed in 1898. Since then, there have been several changes of direction resulting in various revisions of the law. In the last two decades, the evolution seems to have accelerated considerably. While the country's attitude towards intellectual property – especially in the area of counterfeiting – remains ambiguous in some respects, it is in record time that China has established quality procedures and specialized institutions such that high-level professionals have emerged and companies have taken control of the patent.

This quick overview, inevitably partial, underlines the extraordinary capacity of the patent to extend and establish itself durably in countries with varied profiles. In the second half of the 19th century, although its presence and application were not homogeneous throughout the world, the patent already seemed to be on the verge of becoming an almost irreversible standard. Alternative models existed, but they were far from being as successful as the patent.

Let us nevertheless mention the case of the Soviet Union. Indeed, this example is interesting because it proposed an original model more compatible with the communist ideology than the patent. This model was the author's certificate. The conditions for obtaining it were similar to those of a patent. However, a fundamental difference lay in that the Soviet author's certificate was the property of the state. The inventor was paid depending on the use made of their invention. The inventor could also receive other material benefits. Yet in no case could they dispose of their title, for example by transferring or licensing it to a third party. It is interesting to note that even in this peculiar system, the patent was not totally absent, since the inventor actually had the choice of opting for a patent rather than an author's certificate. In practice, however, the vast majority of Soviet inventors were choosing the author's certificate, with patents being filed mostly by foreign inventors. In any case, the anomaly of the author's certificate concluded with the disappearance of the USSR in the early 1990s.

Towards the end of the 19th century, the patent thus largely established itself among the world's major economic powers. Its introduction to countries with different profiles and cultures enriched and improved it, even if differences in approach remained.

The turn of the 19th century was also marked by the expansion of international trade and the beginning of a quest for globalization. The patent, a national tool by nature, risked coming into conflict with this new reality. In order to preserve it, countries would have to work together rather than separately to consider the future of the patent.

WHEN THE WORLD SHRINKS,
THE PATENT EXPANDS

A DREAM OF UNIVERSALITY

THE PARIS CONVENTION, 1883

Signatures and seals on the last page of the Paris Convention of 1883

THE PATENT REACHES
THE TOP OF THE WORLD

WORLD FAIR IN PARIS, 1889

My dear friend,

As promised, I am sending you this letter from Paris. I now understand better why you love this city. You were a thousand times correct: Paris seems to be steeped in history at every corner. When I look at the oldest buildings, I imagine the events that may have taken place there. The last time this happened, at the bend of a street, while I was lost in my daydreams, I thought for a moment that I was face to face with Napoleon! This strange feeling of going back in time is reinforced by the fact that France is celebrating this year the centenary of the storming of the Bastille, which marked the beginning of the Revolution contemporary to ours.

My wife Mina, who accompanied me on this first trip to Europe, also fell in love with the French capital. She wants to see and know everything. We feel an astonishing closeness of heart with these people, yet they are very different from us in many ways.

But it is not so much to discover the past that I came to France... It is with eyes turned to the future and with the firm will to contribute to the progress of humanity that I came here. As you know, Paris is organizing a new World Fair this year. Like the first one, which took place in London in 1851, and the following ones, it is a gigantic event in which many nations will take part (even if the European monarchies have officially refused to participate in this one, to avoid showing support to a revolution that cost King Louis XVI his throne and his head!). Each country came to show the best of its industrial achievements to a public eager to discover novelties that will soon improve the daily lives of us all. As an inventor, it is a pleasure to witness how people rush to see the results of years of research and the fruits of human ingenuity!

The various palaces, galleries and pavilions hosting the exhibition are full of technical and artistic marvels, by which each nation tries to outdo the others. Here, electricity has been deployed on a scale never seen before. My own inventions can be seen both in the United States section and in the Machine Gallery, an architectural gem and a technical feat built specially for the exhibition. My phonograph – a mechanical device I patented in 1877 that uses wax cylinders to record and play back the sound of the voice – seems to be one of the highlights of the exhibition, judging by the number of curious people who flock to see it.

But what impressed Mina and me the most was definitely the Eiffel Tower. I am sure you have heard about it. Seeing this iron colossus of more than 300 meters in height, it is hard to believe that it only took two years to build! It is simply the highest monument in the world, today and probably for decades to come. With this monument, France wanted to show in a brilliant way the quality and the superiority of its technical know-how. I have been told that Parisians were very critical of the aesthetics of the Tower during its construction, but I have noticed, on the contrary, *a great deal of support from the visitors I have met there.*

I thought I would climb the Eiffel Tower like any other visitor. But my fame preceded me and Gustave Eiffel did me the honor of taking me personally to the top of his masterpiece. I will offer him one of my phonographs on occasion to thank him for this touch. Thus, not only the image, but also the voice of this great and audacious engineer will perhaps pass to posterity.

My dear friend, I sincerely hope that you will be able to go to Paris soon to see the Eiffel Tower with your own eyes and admire the view from its top. It is a unique experience that I am sure you will enjoy.

A lavish party was also organized in my honor by the French newspaper Le Figaro, which has a keen interest in science. It took place in a flowered greenhouse filled with electric light and was punctuated by music and various shows. I was touched when, at the end of the evening, a phonograph of my own invention played a message of sympathy for me, introducing me "as one of the princes of this world by right of genius".

I regret that our visit to Paris will soon come to an end. But, in view of the success of the World Fair, I leave with the conviction that technical progress is on the march and that nothing can stop it, for the good of humanity. And the feeling of actively participating in this movement thanks to my inventions gives me immense joy.

I look forward to meeting you and telling you about our journey in person.

Thomas Edison, late August 1889

*

This imaginary letter to a friend could really have been written by the American inventor Thomas Edison, as the details mentioned (including his meeting with Gustave Eiffel) are all true. It highlights the public's infatuation with technical progress in the late 19th century.

At the time, the world was shrinking considerably thanks to the rapid development of new means of communication and lower transportation costs. This movement accelerated the development of international trade. Beyond the purely economic considerations, people of various cultures mixed and understood the interest of exchanging ideas and cooperating with one another. The first attempts at universal unions were made in certain key sectors, such as the telegraph system in 1865 and the postal service in 1874.

It is in this context of attraction to universalism that the World Fairs appeared in the middle of the 19th century. The first of them took place in 1851 in London and aimed to bring the works of industry from all nations together in a single place. The famous Crystal Palace, a huge glass and metal building, was specially designed to accommodate British and foreign exhibitors. Despite the high price of admission, the exhibition was a success, attracting over six million visitors. The event was designed to raise awareness of technical progress and to promote peace and solidarity between peoples. It was also an opportunity for Victorian Britain to show off its industrial and commercial power, then at its peak.

Thereafter, the World Fairs followed one another. The event in 1889, mentioned in Thomas Edison's imaginary letter, was the tenth of its kind and already the fourth to take place in Paris. However, its impact – due in part to the originality of the Eiffel Tower – was great: it attracted 32 million visitors and made a profit of 8 million francs. If Paris is highlighted in this chapter, it is because it is precisely in this city that a new major step in the history of the patent was taken.

World Fairs had an impact on the way patents were perceived. By bringing inventions from all over the world closer to the public, they highlighted the beneficial role of the work of inventors and operators of inventions in the daily lives of everyone. In doing so, they indirectly restored the reputation of patents, which enshrined and protected this work.

At the same time, the World Fairs and the internationalization of trade and industry that they promoted brought about new problems. Indeed, the patent was a national title by nature. As long as trade was essentially local, national protection could suffice to satisfy the needs of inventors and their beneficiaries. But difficulties appeared as soon as one sought to obtain a patent abroad, because that required understanding the procedures of each target country, finding skilled professionals, overcoming language issues and incurring significant costs.

And that is not all: at the end of the 19th century, patent systems still differed widely from country to country. Some still discriminated against foreigners compared to nationals. For example, some countries still required the exploitation of a patented invention within a short period of time (only one year in Austria in 1873, the year of the World Fair in Vienna), at risk of the invalidation of the patent.

In addition, specific problems were created by World Fairs. For example, the public presentation of an invention constituted a disclosure that might have prevented a subsequent patent from being obtained in countries where absolute novelty was a patentability requirement. Moreover, the patent protection offered in some countries organizing World Fairs did not always live up to the expectations of the exhibitors, which presented an even greater risk as imitation and industrial espionage took advantage of these far-reaching events to flourish.

A global patent could solve all of these problems. However, this objective was out of reach as the positions and approaches of the main industrial countries were too far apart. For example, the patent system of the United States was particularly liberal, so much so that the Americans would have liked to align foreign systems with their own. Conversely, other countries such as Germany were not enthusiastic about offering too much protection for fear of being quickly flooded with patents and monopolies granted to American manufacturers. The negotiations held in the run-up to the 1873 Vienna World Fair were unsuccessful.

It was in Paris, host city of the 1878 World Fair, that the discussions resumed. While the United States had dominated the previous negotiations, France's influence logically weighed in on the new agenda. Even as tensions persisted, for example on the question of whether a substantive examination should precede the granting of a patent, the beginnings of a convergence could be seen. The utopian idea of a global patent law was abandoned in favor of a more realistic project of harmonization on only a few consensual points. It was mainly a question of facilitating cooperation between national laws, rather than aligning them completely.

A conference of delegates from twenty powers was convened in March 1883 in Paris to endorse the results of five years of negotiations. Despite the notable absence of the German and Austrian delegates, the conference was a success. The resulting treaty, the Convention for the Protection of Industrial Property, gave birth to the Paris Union (hence the commonly used name "Paris Union Convention", or more simply "Paris Convention"). As its name indicates, the Convention did not only deal with patent law, but with all industrial property rights, including trademarks and designs. It was a treaty open to any State wishing to accede to it.

The two main substantive contributions of the Paris Convention were aimed at solving the problems mentioned above. The first contribution was the "national treatment": according to this rule, each state of the Union would grant the same protection to the nationals of other member states as to its own nationals. Discrimination against foreign applicants, which previously existed in some countries, was thus discouraged within the Union.

The second contribution of the Paris Convention was the "right of priority". This was a legal fabrication according to which, following the filing of a first patent application in a state of the Union, subsequent patent applications filed in other states of the Union for the same invention were considered as having been filed on the date of filing of the first application, provided that the subsequent filings were made within a given period (6 months from the first filing, according to the initial text of the Convention). This principle would allow applicants to organize themselves calmly to undertake the necessary steps abroad, without the risk that the first filings or intermediate disclosures would jeopardize the validity of subsequent patents. In spite of its apparent simplicity, the Union right of priority is in fact surprisingly complex. Many questions about the interpretation and application of this right still arise regularly today.

Beyond these two founding principles, the Paris Convention imposed a certain number of requirements on member states. For example, temporary protection was granted to products presented at World Fairs. Thus, their presentation to the public was no longer considered a novelty-destroying disclosure. Furthermore, the Convention obliged each Member State to set up a national administration specialized in industrial property, which had the effect of further professionalizing the sector and improving the communication of patents to the public.

Despite its boldness, the Paris Convention first gave rise to many reservations. Some countries that mattered in the field of patents, such as the United States and Germany, initially postponed their membership. Elsewhere, anti-unionist movements quickly emerged and denounced the possible abuses of the treaty. This was the case even in France, the cradle of the Union. The Swiss – who did not yet have a patent system at that time, but who nevertheless hosted the International Bureau, the central organ of the Paris Union – were accused of wanting to take advantage of the Convention to impose their monopolies in France without any reciprocity. The mistrust was such that it was feared that the treaty would be terminated at the first revision conference of 1886. Nonetheless, the Paris Union held firm and was quickly joined by a growing number of countries. It also convinced countries that had previously been reluctant, such as Switzerland, to adopt a national patent system, or in the case of the Netherlands, to re-establish one.

Since its creation, the Convention has been revised several times, generally with a view to strengthen the rights of patentees. Among the modifications made to the original text, one can cite the extension of the priority period from 6 to 12 months for patents, the introduction of the principle of independence of patents relating to the same invention (their status and their fate can differ from country to country) and the weakening of the obligation to exploit a patent under penalty of forfeiture. In order for an invention not to be exploited by the patentee to benefit the general public, a compulsory license mechanism was offered, although subject to strict conditions. In the 1934 revision, the "moral" right of inventors to be mentioned as such in patents was recognized. The last modification of the Paris Convention took place in 1979.

In conclusion, even if the Paris Convention remains far from the once cherished dream of establishing a global patent, it is nonetheless a significant step forward in that it initiated the process of transnational harmonization of patent law. Its success has not diminished over time, since it is still in force nearly a century and a half after its initial signing. Today, it has 177 member states, which is a very large part of the planet. In a context of expanding markets, where industrial inventions continue to gain in importance, and of the increasing congestion of patent offices, it quickly became imperative to go further in the standardization of laws to give the patent a supranational status. Europe, in the process of becoming a single market, was to play a leading role in this next development.

COOPERATION AT THE SERVICE OF CREATIVITY

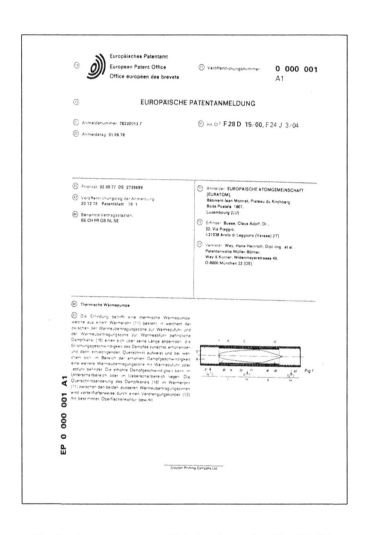

The first European patent, published under number EP 0 000 001 on the 20th of December 1978.

ONE FOR ALL AND ALL FOR ONE!

EUROPEAN PATENT CONVENTION, 1973

The 5ᵗʰ of October 1973, at the Maximilianeum, seat of the Bavarian Parliament in Munich.

The German Kurt Härtel, the French François Savignon and the Dutch Johannes Bob van Benthem are together again. They have been meeting and working together for several years now. Over the years, their personal relationships have grown stronger to the point where they have become friends. Working together creates bonds, especially when it contributes to the fulfillment of a dream, and the three men had dreamt the event they are now living: the signing of the convention that will establish the European Patent Office and create the European patent.

As heads of the patent offices of their respective countries, each became aware very early on of the limits of national patent systems and the difficulties for applicants to protect their inventions in a multitude of countries. They have kept in mind the proposal made to the Council of Europe in 1949 by the French senator and visionary Henri Longchambon to create a

European patent office. At the time, no consensus could be found due to a lack of will and many differences of opinion between states. Even when the creation of the European Economic Community (EEC) in 1957 seemed to offer a new justification for a common patent, the political motivation remained too weak. The tensions around the question of the integration of the United Kingdom into the EEC – to which the France of General de Gaulle had been opposed – had even caused a halt to the on-going technical discussions on the subject.

So, when the idea of a European patent resurfaced in the late 1960s, these three men decided to engage wholeheartedly so that this new opportunity would not be missed again. Putting aside their differences and ignoring their particular interests as much as possible, they worked very hard together. They took part in all the preparatory work and went so far as to hold the key positions at the diplomatic conference of September 1973, set for establishing a European patent convention. There was no shortage of stumbling blocks and tough negotiations were necessary on such difficult issues as the choice of the official language and the location of the future European Patent Office. Nonetheless, the talent and perseverance of these three men paid off in the end, since despite a hundred amendments, the text drafted under the chairmanship of van Benthem was adopted.

On this day of the signing of the convention, François Savignon is taken by a special emotion. He cannot believe that he and his German colleague Härtel fought in enemy camps during the Second World War! However, at this solemn moment, he no longer wants to think about his capture by the Germans nor about his past wounds. He prefers to meditate on the profound significance of the present event and the influence that it will certainly have on the technological future of Europe. From now on, the term "Munich Conference" will no longer be associated with the shame that once led to the dismantling of

Czechoslovakia and plunged Europe into war; it will be the name of a project that brings peace and hope for the future.

As Härtel, Savignon and van Benthem are having a drink, a man approaches them. He congratulates them on their work and, with a smile, tells them that history will remember their names as the "founding fathers" of the European patent. The atmosphere is festive and this remark triggers a general burst of laughter in the small group. To tell the truth, "the three musketeers" would suit them better, since their strength came from their unity. But this is not the time for protest or debate. What matters for the moment is to celebrate the happy outcome of years of hard work. The future will have plenty of time to determine whether the three friends will go down in history... and under what label!

*

The Paris Convention of 1883 had paved the way for a reconciliation of different patent laws, but it had not allowed for the pooling of the means and resources of the member states. A closer cooperation between states was therefore still necessary to cope with the growing number of patents being filed.

At the end of the destructive war of 1939-1945, Europe was exsanguinated and sought to reorganize itself. The big challenges for the reconstruction also created an opportunity for several European countries to work and think about their future together. The first reflections on a European unity, especially for the protection of human rights, led to the creation of the Council of Europe in 1949.

In the patent field as well, the European regional scale quickly appeared to be particularly well suited to effective cooperation between a limited number of states. Moreover, as early as 1947, a pooling of resources had already been initiated between France, Belgium, the Netherlands and Luxembourg. The Hague Agreement had indeed created an International Patent Institute (or IIB after its French name "*Institut International des Brevets*") in charge of conducting prior art searches and giving reasoned opinions on the novelty of inventions that had been the subject of patent applications in one of the member states.

The creation of the Council of Europe provided a new forum for reflection. The Longchambon plan of 1949 – the first attempt to establish a European patent office – was discussed there, before being rejected because of its many imperfections and its premature character. Nevertheless, the discussions that took place within the Council launched a new dynamic. The experts who took part in them continued to explore the paths to European harmonization, even after the rejection of the Longchambon plan.

This continuous work during the 1950s and 1960s led to three conventions, signed in Strasbourg, which standardized certain aspects of patent law. The first, dating from 1953, dealt with formalities applicable to patent applications. A year later, the second convention developed the first version of a so-called international patent classification, aimed at organizing patents according to their technical field. This was a significant step.

The third convention, signed in 1963, was the most ambitious, as it aimed to standardize patent law on two fundamental points: the definition of patentability and the scope of the patent. According to this convention, an invention would be patentable provided that it were new, that it involved an inventive step and that it was susceptible of industrial application. As to the extent of the protection conferred by a patent, it was determined by the claims, while the description and drawings would be used to interpret the claims. This was a major step towards the creation of a European patent, as national practices still differed widely at that time. For example, it is recalled that some European countries, like France, did not yet have inventive step among their patentability criteria and/or required applicants to submit a description but no claims. Other countries, such as the United Kingdom, were still granting national patents for inventions imported from abroad. Although the Strasbourg Convention was not ratified and remained in abeyance for more than a decade, the harmonization it established would later serve as the basis for the emergence of the European patent.

It is quite striking to note how early the first attempts to organize a patent for all of Europe were made. The Longchambon plan and the discussions that followed it in the Council of Europe preceded by several years the Treaty of Rome that established the EEC in 1957. They started even before the creation of the European Coal and Steel Community (ECSC) in 1951! This shows that the patent was already perceived as an important economic and political tool at the time. However, it was the creation of an economic body for Europe that gave the necessary impetus to the completion of the project for a common patent.

With the creation of the EEC, a common market was born. By providing a customs union, the EEC aimed to eliminate the economic borders that divided Europe. This logic of openness, where goods and services must circulate freely, is in direct conflict with that of patents, whose national character requires the maintenance of barriers between states. Only a supranational patent holding authority in several states would be able to resolve this contradiction. From this perspective, a unitary patent within the European Community would make the most sense. However, the Council of Europe, which had supervised the previous discussions, considered things from a different angle and had a broad conception of Europe going beyond the borders of the six founding members of the EEC (West Germany, Belgium, Luxembourg, the Netherlands, France and Italy).

In order to preserve both approaches, it was therefore decided in 1969 that several objectives should be pursued in parallel: on the one hand, the creation of a European patent obtained at the end of a common grant procedure under the supervision of a European patent office and equivalent to a bundle of national patents in a group of states not limited to the EEC; on the other, the establishment of a true unitary patent, i.e. a single title covering only the member states of the EEC. Conducting these negotiations simultaneously offered the hope of a more rapid outcome for each project. There was indeed urgency because another cooperation project pushed by the United States was about to become a reality. This project, called the Patent Cooperation Treaty or PCT, which will be discussed in the next chapter, was certainly less ambitious than the European projects, although it was intended to be global. As a result, some European countries feared that it would threaten their interests. This led Europe to take the initiative.

An intergovernmental conference was held in Luxembourg in early 1969 to make progress on the idea of the European patent. It brought together the six EEC states as well as a number of invited third countries, such as Turkey. While some of the invited countries chose not to participate, other states that had not initially been invited were finally admitted to the conference. Israel, on the other hand, which had expressed interest in joining the discussions, was not allowed to do so. The "founding fathers" mentioned above participated actively in the numerous working sessions that spanned more than two years. Their involvement, as well as that of the experts and future users involved in the discussions, was a major factor in the success of the conference. Thanks to their hard work, the European Patent Convention (EPC) was signed in Munich on the 5th of October 1973.

To achieve such a result, several difficulties had to be overcome and important concessions had to be made. As mentioned in the story above, the subjects of the official languages and the seat of the future European Patent Office were among the most sensitive. As a trade-off, three official languages were finally adopted on an equal basis: German, English and French. As for the seat of the European Patent Office, it was determined to be Munich, a city that already hosted the German national office whose expertise in patent examination was recognized. A department of the European Patent Office was also created in The Hague, continuing from the IIB. The other cities that had applied to host the seat – London and Nice – were rejected, depriving the future staff of the office the prospect of working on the banks of the Thames or the sunny shores of the Mediterranean Sea.

The EPC came into full force in November 1977. The European Patent Office (EPO) opened its doors with a limited staff. Bob van Benthem was its first president. The European patent application EP 0 000 001 was published in December 1978, the same day as about hundred other applications. It was filed, in the German language, by the European Atomic Energy Community (Euratom) and concerned a thermal heat pump. It led to the issuance of a European patent in January 1981.

The creation of the European patent constituted a major development in the history of patents because it implied not only a mutualization of means and a broad harmonization of substantive law, but it went so far as to establish a common legal title directly applicable in all or some of the member states of the EPC. Part of the sovereignty of these states – the capacity to issue legal titles – was thus abandoned in favor of a central and independent institution, the EPO. How far we have come from the days when patents were granted in a local and arbitrary manner at the whim of a monarch!

It should nevertheless be recalled that the EPC was not the first treaty to establish a unified law and a supranational organization: the African and Malagasy Industrial Property

Office indeed preceded the EPO. Created by the Treaty of Libreville, which was devised in 1962 between twelve newly independent French-speaking African States, it was charged with issuing a patent title applicable in each of the member states according to a single procedure. Following a revision in 1977, it became the African Intellectual Property Organization (or OAPI after its French name "*Organisation Africaine de la Propriété Intellectuelle*").

Forty years after the grant of the first European patent, the success of the system established by the EPC is undeniable. The EPO now has 38 member states – the 27 member states of the European Union and other countries such as Norway, Switzerland and Turkey. Bilateral cooperation agreements also allow third countries, such as Morocco, Tunisia or Cambodia, to offer national protection on the basis of a European patent. The European patent system thus covers a total population of almost 700 million people. The EPO is the European organization with the largest number of employees, aside from the European Union institutions. The quality of the examinations and oppositions carried out under the supervision of its more than 4,000 engineers in all technical fields is often praised well beyond the borders of Europe. The EPO services are used by non-European companies, not only to obtain European patents, but also to carry out approximately 30% of the world's prior art searches under the PCT.

The creation of the European patent has also given rise to a new profession: the European patent attorney, who is the only one (along with lawyers) entitled to represent natural or legal persons before the EPO. This is a rare, perhaps even unique, example of a profession that is totally integrated and harmonized on a large supranational scale. Every year, candidates from the 38 EPO member states simultaneously take the same qualification exam in the hope of joining this technical-legal profession, which currently has approximately 12,500 members. The practical possibilities offered by this profession – working on an equal footing with counterparts from various countries, in an environment where cultures and native languages differ but where all share the common language of the EPC and the universal language of science and technology – can be considered a *tour de force*.

The success of the European patent should not, however, conceal its limitations. The main one is certainly that, after being granted, European patents are assimilated with national patents and thus become fully governed by the specific law of each state where they are in force. Despite some rare common provisions, the validity and infringement of a European patent remain within the competence of national jurisdictions, which judge according to their own law and their body of national case law. Questions as fundamental as how to interpret the scope of the claims – literally or flexibly, structurally or functionally, etc. – are still subject to diverse practices that vary between countries. This explains why the holder of a European patent must bring a multitude of lawsuits before courts with the assistance of local lawyers – and incur the corresponding costs! – if they want to stop a pan-European infringement. This occasionally leads to a troublesome phenomenon: the rendering of irreconcilable decisions between countries, whereby the exact same European patent can be judged, for example, invalid in the United Kingdom, valid and infringed in France, and valid but not infringed in Germany.

Over the years, Europe has nevertheless developed instruments that improve legal certainty for users. For example, the Brussels Convention of 1968 and subsequent legal texts have established common rules of general application concerning court jurisdiction, recognition and enforcement of judgments in civil and commercial matters. These rules have introduced some order to the organization of legal actions susceptible to be brought in several countries. In the field of patents, they theoretically apply to actions of infringement or invalidity. However, they remain insufficient, being powerless to resolve a fundamental problem: after being granted, a European patent is nothing more than a bundle of national patents, independent of each other.

Only a unitary patent, i.e. a single title conferring truly uniform protection throughout – or almost throughout – the European Union, accompanied by a unified court, would make it possible to offer protection compatible with the concept of a single market. It would theoretically simplify access to geographically broad protection and would make it possible to better assess in advance the scope of one's own patents as well as those of third parties.

The work on the unitary patent, started in parallel with that of the European patent, also resulted in a legal text: the 1975 Luxembourg Convention. Despite the many advantages it offered, this type of patent was not able to win the support of the states concerned. The Luxembourg Convention never obtained the ratifications necessary for its entry into force.

More recently though, the unitary patent has returned to the forefront, with a new project initiated in the context of enhanced cooperation within the European Union. According to this project, the unitary patent will be based on the European patent granted by the EPO according to the provisions of the EPC, which makes it possible to take advantage of existing procedures that have proved their worth. Once the European patent is granted, the owner will be able to opt for unitary effect in order to obtain uniform protection in all participating EU countries.

In parallel, on the judicial front, a draft international agreement of 2013 has defined a Unified Patent Court (UPC). If it comes to life (which seems within reach at the time of writing), this specialized court will have exclusive jurisdiction to hear disputes relating to unitary patents as well as European patents. This project, which is complex by nature, suggests that the participating states give up a substantial part of their sovereignty in a sensitive economic field. It is therefore understandable that some people have reservations about it. These reservations have given rise to initiatives, including several (ultimately rejected) constitutional challenges in Germany, which have put the project on hold for a long time and led to fears that it would be completely stopped. In addition, like when it entered the EEC at the time, the United Kingdom, which recently left the EU, also came to thwart the progress of the UPC and the unitary patent by suddenly depriving the EU of about one-eighth of its total population and one of its most developed markets. However, though slightly less attractive under these circumstances, the UPC and unitary patent projects have not been stopped by Brexit.

The next few months and years will undoubtedly be decisive. The advent, which seems imminent at the time of writing, of a unitary title and a unified judicial institution will mark the end of a wait of almost half a century. It will represent a major new step in the construction of an integrated Europe. There is no doubt that the first rulings of the UPC will be scrutinized by observers from all over the world. At a time when doubts and criticism of the European Union are commonplace, it is crucial for its success that the UPC be staffed with outstanding judges, capable of issuing high quality, clear and fair decisions. If successful, it will have accomplished one of the most ambitious achievements in the history of the patent.

PCT

WORLD INTELLECTUAL PROPERTY ORGANIZATION
International Bureau

INTERNATIONAL APPLICATION PUBLISHED UNDER THE PATENT COOPERATION TREATY (PCT)

51) International Patent Classification: C03B 19/00 C03C 3/00, 11/00	A1	(11) International Publication Number: WO 78/00001
		(43) International Publication Date: 19 October 1978 (19.10

21) International Application Number: PCT/US78/00002

22) International Filing Date: 1 June 1978 (01.06.78)

31) Priority Application Numbers: 827,725 894,188

32) Priority Dates: 25 August 1977 (25.08.77) 6 April 1978 (06.04.78)

33) Priority Country: US

71) Applicant: SAMANTA, Mrinmay; Post Office Box 2322, Washington D.C. 20013, United States of America.

(72) Inventor: Applicant is also the inventor.

(81) Designated States: BR, CH, CH (regional patent), DE, DE (regional patent), FR (regional patent) GB, GB (regional patent), LU (regional patent) SE, SE (regional patent), SU .

Published before the expiration of the time limit referred in Article 21(2)(a) on the request of the applicant, with *International search report.*

The applicant has declared that he does not wish to amen the claims of his international application under Article

(54) Title: LOW TEMPERATURE SYNTHESIS OF VITREOUS BODIES AND THEIR INTERMEDIATES

(57) Abstract

A method of making glass of high purity and in virtually unlimited shapes via solution deposition on a porous self supporting body by reaction between a first solution and a second solution; and a product made thereby. The first solu tion containing at least one basic glass forming solute is confined within a porous container, the walls of which are substan tially impermeable to the basic solute. The second solution containing at least one acidic solute is diffused into the porou container through its walls which are substantially permeable to the said acidic solute. The reaction between the first solu tion and the second solution takes place within the porous container leading to the deposition of a self-supporting porou body on the inside walls of the container. The porous body which is crystalline, vitreous or intermediate between the two is purified by leaching and/or washing, dried and thermally consolidated, to a transparent non-porous glass.

The first PCT application, published under number WO7800001 on the 19th of October 1978

Time is Money

Patent Cooperation Treaty, 1970

The First World War brought an abrupt end to thirty years of growth in the number of patent filings worldwide. After three more decades of stagnation, the end of World War II marked the beginning of a new phase of strong growth. The number of patent applications filed quadrupled between 1946 and 1973, going from about 200,000 to 800,000.

This increase can be explained in part by the return of peace, which benefitted international trade. Applicants were no longer protecting their inventions only in their local market, but stepped up with filings abroad. Even in the heart of Western Europe, the share of patents originating from abroad was about to become the majority. This phenomenon was all the more significant given that patent applications were filed less and less by individual inventors with limited resources and more and more by dynamic companies set out to conquer new markets.

This trend both revealed the imperfections of the existing patent systems and created new problems. First, for the applicants, the geographical expansion of their activities obliged them to take steps in a large number of countries within a period of twelve months (the priority deadline defined by the Paris Convention), which proved to be too short and inadequate a timeframe. This created a time and budget pressure for applicants, since official fees and outside counsel fees increased with the number of countries where protection was sought.

As for the national patent offices, they had become victims of their own success. The influx of patent applications was becoming overwhelming and disrupted their operations. Delays were accumulating dangerously, in particular in countries conducting a substantive examination of the patent applications. This situation was all the more unsatisfactory because the work of the various offices was partly redundant, especially with regard to formalities. Moreover, the multiple searches and examinations conducted in parallel by different offices led to results that were not always homogeneous. Substantial change became necessary to prevent the system from collapsing.

In the mid-1960s, when discussions to establish a regional patent in Europe were stalled, the United States took initiative and decided to seek a solution to the above-mentioned problems. Coordinating with the other countries that mattered in the field of patents, they devised a new form of cooperation. The task of preparing a draft convention to implement this initiative was entrusted to a new intergovernmental organization, based in Switzerland: the World Intellectual Property Office (WIPO).

Replacing the former *Bureaux internationaux réunis pour la protection de la propriété intellectuelle* (BIRPI), which had administered the Paris Convention (as well as the Berne Convention for the Protection of Literary and

Artistic Works) since 1893, WIPO was officially created by a 1967 Convention, which entered into force on the 26th of April 1970. In remembrance of this event, World Intellectual Property Day is celebrated on the 26th of April to raise public awareness of intellectual property issues and to pay tribute to the work of creators and inventors from around the world.

WIPO's primary mission is to promote and develop the protection of intellectual property in the broadest sense throughout the world. It is responsible for defending the interests of both industrialized countries and developing countries, which must be able to find in intellectual property, and in patents in particular, a means to catch up. To reinforce its international vocation, WIPO became a specialized agency of the UN in 1974. Today, WIPO administers no less than 26 treaties dealing with all aspects of intellectual property, including patents, trademarks, designs and copyright. One of these treaties, which is of particular interest to us here, is commonly referred to as the PCT, which stands for Patent Cooperation Treaty.

It is indeed this treaty that WIPO was charged with preparing at the end of the 1960s in order to improve worldwide cooperation in patents. This work, in which economic actors were involved, quickly produced results. The PCT treaty was signed in Washington in 1970.

How does the PCT mark a significant progress in the world of patents? By creating the new concept of an "international application" (or "PCT application"). An international application is a single application, drafted in a single language and filed with a single Receiving Office, which has the effect of a regular national patent application in each of the countries selected by the applicant (the "designated" or "elected" states). Only one filing is therefore necessary to cover a multitude of countries and to obtain a single filing date, recognized everywhere at the same time. This is its first major simplification.

However, the PCT goes even further by subjecting the international application to a first procedural stage called the international phase, during which it is subject to an international search. The latter is in fact a prior art search carried out centrally by a competent authority (International Search Authority or ISA) which is generally an authorized national or regional patent office. The international search report and the written opinion issued by the ISA provide the applicant with relevant indications on the patentability of their invention, at an early stage and for a limited cost. In addition, the applicant has the opportunity to amend the claims of their application to take into account the results of the international search, for example by narrowing the claim scope and thus better distinguishing it from a prior art that is too close.

The PCT application is subject to an international publication. In addition, an optional substantive examination can be carried out at the request of applicants during the international phase. This international preliminary examination allows applicants to strengthen the patentability of their invention via a dialogue with a specialized examiner of a competent authority (International Preliminary Examining Authority or IPEA).

It is only at the end of the international phase – at least 30 months from the filing date of the PCT application (or of the earliest application whose priority is claimed) – that the applicant must perform acts before national offices in order to obtain protection in the countries they have selected. The application then enters the second part of its life, the so-called national phase. Among the steps to be taken at this stage are the submission of a translation of the application and the payment of fees to each of the offices of the selected countries. In this way, most of the costs of protection are deferred, illustrating the adage that "time is money". This is especially true since the time saved before incurring the main costs allows the applicant to strengthen the patentability of their invention and to better assess their ability to make it a successful innovation.

Granting national patents from a PCT application remains a prerogative of individual states. During the national phases, the offices of the designated states are indeed free to carry out their own examination. Therefore, a favorable international search or examination does not guarantee the grant of a patent in the end. In many cases, however, the international phase simplifies the work and reduces the uncertainty during the subsequent national phases.

As we can see, the PCT application is still far from what would be a global patent, with each country remaining in control of granting or declining a patent according to its own procedure and evaluation criteria. Nevertheless, its international phase comes close by simplifying and centralizing several key milestones.

Another remarkable element of the PCT is to be found, as its name suggests, in the new possibilities of cooperation between states that it offers. For example, it is now possible for an American citizen to file a PCT application with the United States Patent Office, to request the establishment of an international search by the European Patent Office, and to take advantage of the search results to obtain a patent in China!

This cooperation has strengthened over time, with new possibilities being regularly introduced into the PCT to offer ever greater flexibility to applicants. For instance, for some years now, it has been possible to request multiple international searches from several offices for the same PCT application, which increases the chances of identifying, at an early stage, the most relevant prior art. The PCT is often a pioneer in developing new rules of law, which are sometimes adopted later on in the national laws of various countries.

The PCT may seem complex, but its complexity is largely the result of the flexibility offered by the system. This flexibility allows the contracting states to choose whether or not to implement certain provisions, so as to remain consistent with their national law. It is a flexibility that also allows informed or well advised applicants to implement "tailor-made" strategies that fit their needs as closely as possible.

The PCT and the European Patent Convention (EPC) have sometimes been referred to as twin treaties. It is true that they came to life at roughly the same time and that both are concerned with greater cooperation between states. Despite their similarities, however, twins sometimes develop a form of rivalry: the PCT and the EPC are no exception to this principle. Despite the unprecedented prospects offered by the PCT, this treaty initially aroused the mistrust of certain European countries, like France.

In the 1960s, the French grant procedure did not include an examination of patent applications. France therefore feared that the PCT would cause it to lose influence by giving preference to countries with examination. There was indeed a risk that French applicants would have to rely on international searches performed by foreign offices, such as those of Germany or the United States, to obtain patents in France. The quick creation of a European patent office granting patents after a robust examination was therefore pushed by France, in order to become a bulwark at the gates of the European patent system. The International Patent Institute (the IIB, a future component of the EPO mentioned in the previous chapter) was quickly proposed and accepted to be one of the authorities in charge of the international search within the framework of the PCT. Today, a good part of the international searches are carried out by the EPO. Cooperation thus seems to have prevailed over the rivalry of yesteryear.

The PCT came into force in 1978 and quickly took off. While it is far from having eliminated direct filings with national offices, it has become a common means of protection for many patent holders around the world. In 2020, the number of international applications filed since the PCT started 40 years ago has reached almost 4 million. The number of contracting states to the PCT currently stands at 154, which includes all industrialized countries, with the notable exception of Argentina.

Although the PCT provided a new, open and common route to patenting for almost all applicants worldwide, it has only marginally influenced national laws. Patents granted by states, even on the basis of the same international application, remain subject to different regimes. However, towards the end of the 20th century, knowledge and innovation have been taking an increasing part in the value of products and services marketed throughout the world. The different levels of protection offered, depending on the country, for these intangible assets have created tensions in international economic relations. In order to ease these tensions, it is from the perspective of international trade that patents would experience the next – and to date, last – major step in their evolution.

THE COMMON LANGUAGE OF TRADE

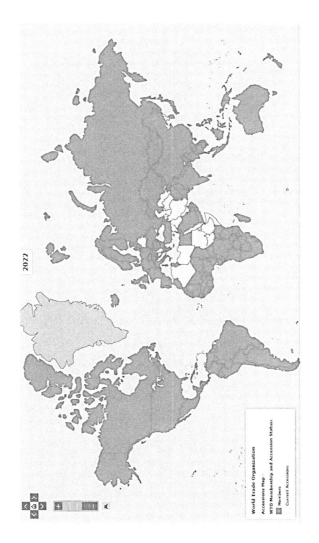

WTO members and current accessions

There are not many countries excluded.

A UNIVERSAL MINIMUM STANDARD
FOR THE BENEFIT OF ALL?

AGREEMENT ON TRADE-RELATED ASPECTS
OF INTELLECTUAL PROPERTY RIGHTS, 1994

Since the creation of the General Agreement on Tariffs and Trade (GATT) in 1947, multilateral discussions on free trade and tariffs have been held regularly. The last round of these discussions, the Uruguay Round, gave birth to a new international institution in 1995: the World Trade Organization (WTO). Among the many agreements that accompanied the creation of the WTO was one on Trade-Related Aspects of Intellectual Property Rights (TRIPS).

With the TRIPS Agreement pushed by the United States, WTO member states recognized the importance of the links between intellectual property and trade. In order to allow international trade to flourish, the Agreement established a minimum standard of intellectual property protection to be met by all WTO members.

This represented a paradigm shift. For the most part, the prior multilateral patent agreements mentioned in the previous chapters were technical treaties creating additional rights to address specific problems. For instance, they worked towards improving the situation of foreign nationals, facilitating the procedures for applicants, reducing the administrative burden, and so on. Without replacing the previous treaties, the TRIPS Agreement took a different approach by seeking to put intellectual property at the service of higher objectives. It thus focused on the function of the patent rather than on its form. This approach required member states to adapt their national patent laws.

Article 7 of the Agreement summarizes the objectives well. It states that "the protection and enforcement of intellectual property rights should contribute to the promotion of technological innovation and to the transfer and dissemination of technology, to the mutual advantage of producers and users of technological knowledge and in a manner conducive to social and economic welfare, and to a balance of rights and obligations". The agreement was thus conceived as a means to advance all parties. It was intended to be balanced by conferring benefits to the developers of technical innovations (through respect for intellectual property) as well as to the users of these innovations (through technology transfer). Industrialized countries intended to use the agreement to push their technological advantage, while developing countries hoped it would help them to catch up. This hope was based on concrete provisions, as Article 66 of the agreement states that developed countries shall provide incentives to their enterprises and institutions to promote and encourage technology transfer to less developed countries in order to enable them to build a sound and viable technological base. Developing countries were also given long, extendable deadlines to bring their laws into compliance with TRIPS (e.g. until 2016 to grant patents on pharmaceuticals).

What principles did the TRIPS Agreement introduce to the field of intellectual property? First of all, it strengthened the fight against discrimination. The Agreement reaffirmed the principle of "national treatment", which secured the equal treatment of foreigners and nationals as was already set out in the Paris Convention. It also contributed a principle known as "most-favored-nation treatment", which imposes equal treatment between all WTO states so that an advantage granted to the nationals of one country must immediately be extended to the nationals of all other member states.

With regard to patents, TRIPS set a minimum standard on several fundamental issues. In particular, the term of protection was set to a minimum of 20 years from the date of filing (which was not yet the case in the United States). Concerning substance, patents must be available for any inventions, whether products or processes, in all fields of technology, which constitutes an almost complete expansion of the scope of the patents. Only a limited number of exceptions to patentability were provided for to protect *ordre public* or morality by excluding diagnostic, therapeutic and surgical methods, or plants and animals. The requirement that any patent must describe the invention in a manner sufficiently clear and complete for it to be carried out by a person skilled in the art is also stated. These principles were taken or derived from pre-existing legislation.

In addition to these characteristics of the patent, the agreement further harmonized its effects. The acts prohibited to third parties were listed precisely: making, using, offering for sale, selling or importing a patented product or any product obtained directly by a patented process. The Agreement also established the right to assign or license a patent. In the case of abuse of rights by the patentee, the Agreement allowed for the overriding of rights by issuing conditional "compulsory licenses", through which a third party can produce or use the subject matter of the patent without the authorization of the owner. The delicate question of whether compulsory licenses can be used by member states to protect public health was positively resolved in 2001 at the Doha Ministerial Conference.

Perhaps the most important contribution of the TRIPS Agreement was that it not only sought to define the contours of intellectual property rights, but also addressed the means of enforcing those rights. This was a first that had far-reaching implications. This part of the agreement obliges member states to ensure, through fair and equitable procedures, an effective fight against any infringement of intellectual property rights on their territory. To this end, countries have a complete arsenal at their disposal: procedures for obtaining evidence, provisional measures (to prevent infringement or to preserve evidence), injunctions (to order a party to desist from an infringement), payment of damages by the infringer, as well as other remedies. The application and enforcement of these measures remain, of course, within the jurisdiction of national courts of the member states. Nonetheless, their adoption at the WTO level – currently comprising 164 member states – marked a significant step towards a kind of global patent governance.

In fact, the scope of TRIPS is such that it is difficult today to imagine going much further. Since the basic principles have now been harmonized, taking additional steps would mean agreeing on all the details, doing away with the last local specificities and suppressing the share of national sovereignty that the states still have to freely dispose of their patents. In other words, it would mean setting up a global patent and a related court system. Aside from the European project of a unitary patent, which nevertheless remains regional, this objective seems out of reach for the foreseeable future.

Indeed, while reconciling laws on some aspects, the TRIPS Agreement has highlighted fundamental differences between countries. Some, like the Nobel Prize-winning economist Joseph E. Stiglitz, believe that TRIPS has imposed an American-European model on the world that is unsuitable for developing countries. Moreover, TRIPS has generated a variety of frustrations. Developing countries have felt that the agreement offers strong protection to the great powers, without resulting in the benefit of technology transfer or the influx of investment expected in return. On the other hand, some developed countries would like to see a stricter application of the agreement and a limited use of any provision that could restrict the rights of patent holders.

Recently, bilateral trade agreements have been used as a vehicle to strengthen intellectual property protection. Rules going beyond the TRIPS minimum standard have been imposed on countries in weak trade positions, such as terms of protection longer than 20 years, the limited use of compulsory licenses, or other provisions favorable to patent holders. The term "TRIPS Plus" is sometimes used to refer to these practices that use bilateralism in order to obtain conditions that multilateralism cannot offer.

Moreover, even between industrial powers, tensions are emerging over patent disputes and accusations of intellectual property theft. The ultra-dominance of the United States is now being challenged by new powers, such as China. It is not certain that these countries still have an interest in common standards. Until now, international patent treaties have been encouraged by the United States and Europe to establish their technological dominance. Will the same be true in a more multipolar world?

Do these recent developments put a stop to the international process that started in the 19th century and has seen the various patent legislations getting closer and closer over time? Perhaps, and at least in the sole multilateral form we have seen so far.

But does this mean that we have reached the end of the history of patents? Nothing is less certain.

Since the Venetian guilds, the privileges of Queen Elizabeth I, the tactics of Minister Colbert, through to the American Constitution, the European hesitations, and up to the internationalization of the law, patents have shown an extraordinary capacity to adapt up to the times. Without ever achieving unanimity, they have been able to endure the centuries. But like our societies, of which they are a reflection, they are currently facing totally new challenges. After our journey into the past, it is now time to look at the present and open a window onto the future of the patent.

PART 2

THE PATENT
IN THE 21ST CENTURY

A HISTORY IN THE MAKING

JUSTIFYING THE PATENT

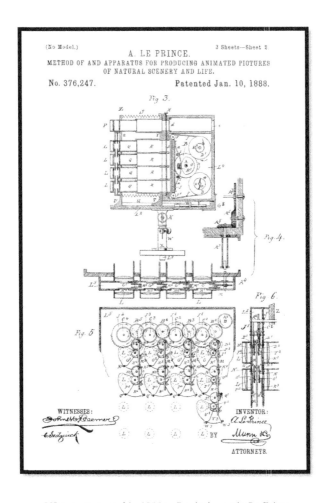

US patent granted in 1888 to Louis Augustin Le Prince
for a photographic camera to produce animated images

Le Prince mysteriously disappeared on a train in 1890, just as he was
about to give the first cinematographic demonstration in history.
Three years later, Edison demonstrated his kinetoscope.
Could Edison have him murdered to steal his invention,
as Le Prince's family claimed?

Source: Espacenet - Public domain

Information: A good like no other

Buying a car, renting an apartment, subscribing to a newspaper. All of these activities seem completely natural to us. It would never occur to anyone to question their foundations by, for example, making use of any of these goods while refusing to pay the price. Such premises have become more complicated, however, with the advent of digital technologies that dematerialize a number of aspects of our lives. Consumers have become accustomed to being offered services for free – or seemingly for free – that they would otherwise have been willing to pay a great deal for in the old world. Consider, for example, our use of countless news feeds, services for connecting people and applications that deliver audio or video content. Despite this shift, the idea remains in our minds that in order to personally benefit from a quality product or service, it is logical to pay the provider thereof.

This logic is challenged as soon as one approaches the domain of abstraction and of creations of the mind. If, as the adage attributed to law Professor Henri Desbois, "ideas are free to travel" ("*les idées sont de libre parcours*"), should their concrete expressions in the form of creations not be shared by all? In the world of technology, should an invention not be freely adopted by as many stakeholders as possible in order to benefit the greatest number of users, like a common good?

To answer these questions, it is necessary to characterize works of the mind, and, more particularly, inventions. First of all, inventions have something in common with material goods: they do not come out of nowhere, but are the result of substantial work, even if this work is intellectual rather than physical in nature. Since the work of transforming an idea or a discovery into a concrete technical achievement is useful to society, it deserves to be compensated for, just as a product made with tools does.

The process of creation is complex, and the motivations of inventors vary from one individual to another and according to the particular context in which their ideas evolve. While some inventors are essentially driven by curiosity and the desire to solve a problem, others are more sensitive to the prospect of being recognized by their peers or of making a fortune. In addition, those working in a company are simply given a mission to invent, be it alone or in a group. Beyond motivations, the means of arriving at an innovation are rarely linear and often move back and forth between abstract and concrete phases. The most elaborate creations nevertheless share the fact that they are generally the product of long-term work. This work often begins with a period of prior learning, during which the creators acquire knowledge that enables them to improve that which already exists. According to Pasteur's words, "luck favors only the prepared minds". Thus, in spite of an undeniable degree of innate genius, Wolfgang Amadeus Mozart would probably not have produced the same operas if his father Leopold had not introduced him to music very early and had not known how to make the most of his natural gifts. Likewise, Einstein would certainly never have had the idea of his theory of relativity, nor would he have filed patents on numerous devices, if he had not first studied mathematics and physics for years. This is not to minimize the role of natural ability; people who cannot read music can sometimes compose or reproduce beautiful melodies by ear, and people without scientific training can design ingenious systems. However, the development of a sophisticated invention is most often based on a foundation of prior knowledge, just as raw materials are needed to make a manufactured object. All this work, from learning to improving that which already exists, is indirectly reflected in the final invention and should therefore be valued, despite its purely intellectual nature.

If inventions resemble material goods in that they result from work, they can be distinguished from them by other characteristics. By their very nature, inventions – which are not to be confused with the physical objects they make possible to produce – are information. Any invention can indeed be described in words as a combination of technical features (as is expressed in patent claims). An inventor who publicly describes their invention immediately loses control of it, since it can then be copied by any skilled person. In other words, the disclosed invention cannot be appropriated by its creator. Nor is it possible to withdraw knowledge of a disclosed invention *ex post* from anyone who has acquired it. This characteristic of non-appropriability encourages the inventor to keep their inventions secret rather than disclose them and risk having them exploited by others. This is why the old guilds were so keen to keep secret the techniques developed by their members, as we have seen above.

Nonetheless, the secrecy of inventions is not maintained without consequences. It hinders technical progress by depriving future generations of inventors of a raw material that is essential to making possible improvements. It also prevents the transfer of technology, because it is impossible to generate sufficient interest in an invention from a potential buyer without revealing the technical details of the product. This problem is known as the Arrow's paradox: if I want to sell information to a third party, I have to communicate it at least partially, but this communication makes it instantly lose its value, thus rendering the sale impossible.

Another property of the invention is that it is a so-called "non-rival" good. In other words, unlike most material goods, an invention can be used by several people simultaneously without deteriorating. According to Thomas Jefferson's image mentioned earlier, the invention is indeed like a candle that does not lose its luster when it lights another. Jefferson used this metaphor to explain that the invention should be able to proliferate freely. However, the fact that the invention is equally accessible to all, not just those who pay to access it, poses an economic problem. A potential buyer has no incentive to invest in an object that others can obtain at no cost and whose diffusion cannot be effectively controlled.

In summary, inventors (and their successors in title) are entitled to expect remuneration for the inventions they make available to the public. However, the difficulties they face when it comes to appropriating and commercializing their inventions can dissuade them from starting a creative process. As a result, the natural incentive to keep their inventions secret may prevent other inventors from improving them. This dual barrier to innovation, which acts upon the present and the future, ultimately performs a disservice to society because it deprives us of new products and services capable of improving daily life.

As an informational object, the invention demands a unique approach so as to solve the above-mentioned problems. Does this approach involve patents?

Geneva Treaty on the International Recording of Scientific Discoveries

Adopted at Geneva on March 3, 1978

World Intellectual Property Organization
GENEVA 1978

Geneva Treaty on the International Recording of Scientific Discoveries,
1978

Utility vs. Morality

Two opposing approaches are generally used to justify the existence of the patent. Nowadays, this divide is regularly expressed in controversies between supporters of the two camps. However, it already existed in the early patent laws mentioned above, in which either of the two approaches appeared depending on the country and the period.

The first approach is called deontological, i.e. moral. In this approach, copying an invention without the inventor's consent is reprehensible, regardless of the economic consequences. Copying is equated to theft. This approach presupposes that the inventor has some form of ownership over their invention. This relates to the idea of an inventor's natural right – an idea that supported important changes made to the English patent system in the 18th century and was introduced into French law in 1791 by the Knight of Boufflers. The purpose of the patent would therefore be to protect the inventor's property in their work.

As we have seen, the natural right of inventors is a difficult position to defend because of its absolutist stance.

Taken to the extreme, the logic of this natural right cannot be applied to an ownership that is not unlimited in time. This difficulty led France to remove it from law in 1844. However, the inventor's merit was not totally erased; the patent has been transformed from a property right into a tool that rewards the inventor's efforts. Today, this vision is widespread, since inventors are named as such in patents all over the world. Even when they are simply employees of companies rather than the applicants, inventors benefit from a specific remuneration for their inventions in many countries.

Without being totally broken, the natural link between the inventor and their invention has progressively become more tenuous. Regularly, new provisions further weaken this once sacred bond. For example, the *America Invents Act*, a U.S. law made in 2016, allowed companies to file U.S. patents in their own names rather than in the inventors' names, as was previously required. Similarly, the European Patent Office recently stopped notifying inventors of the details of patent applications designating them as such, limiting its channels of communication to the applicants. While these changes may seem trivial and simplify the process to the benefit of companies, they illustrate the fact that the inventor has been moved into the background.

One of the best indications that the moral approach alone can no longer explain the existence of the patent is to be found in the field not of inventions, but of scientific discoveries. Discoveries bring to light pre-existing phenomena, whereas inventions bring to life something that did not previously exist. Despite their fundamental character, discoveries have never been the subject of legal protection. Attempts to establish such a right for scientists have all failed. A treaty providing for a simple international registration of scientific discoveries was adopted in Geneva in 1978, but never came into force. If the intellectual effort of theorists is insufficient to justify a right to their discoveries, it is because the deepest motivation for patent law lies elsewhere, namely in the field of economics.

This is the approach taken by the second, so-called utilitarian (or consequentialist) approach. This approach, which is more pragmatic and rational, is focused on the economic effects of innovation. It tries to justify the existence of the patent on the basis of its overall cost/benefit ratio. The utilitarian approach has been at the heart of the American patent system since its inauguration. In this respect, it is worth noting again that the first article of the United States Constitution enshrined the principle of exclusive rights granted to inventors in the interest of promoting the scientific progress.

The question asked by the utilitarian approach thus concerns whether the positive economic consequences of a patent policy outweigh its negative consequences. In particular, it considers whether the patent is able to solve the problems inherent to the informational nature of the invention, as mentioned in the previous chapter.

On a theoretical level, this seems to be the case. Indeed, by defining an exclusive right of the inventor to their invention, the patent establishes a form of appropriation; copying becomes forbidden without the inventor's consent and can be sanctioned by the courts. It enables one to control the uses of the invention, thus introducing an element of rivalry into the space of intangible assets. Once appropriation is guaranteed, the incentive for the inventor to keep their inventions secret is no longer relevant. Knowledge can spread more freely, especially since access to technical information is facilitated by the publication of patents. Moreover, the inventor, who filed a patent application, has no more issues around communicating the details of their invention to a potential buyer. As such, by solving the Arrow's paradox, patents theoretically improve the circulation of ideas and the transfer of technologies.

While the utilitarian justification of the patent may seem pertinent at first glance, it has many weaknesses. Indeed, it is impossible to evaluate precisely all the economic consequences of patenting. For example, what proportion of the inventions made would be really kept secret in the absence of a patent system, and what proportion of the inventions remain secret despite the existence of a patent system? It is difficult to know, and the answer to these questions probably varies widely from country to country, industry to industry, and even from one company to another.

Moreover, because of divergent interests between stakeholders, what are deemed positive economic consequences for some may in fact prove negative for others. An overall assessment can only be made from a given perspective, depending on the point of view from which one is looking. Utility is thus relative. In addition, the roles of the various stakeholders are sometimes ambivalent. For example, an inventor who has a patent protecting their invention may simultaneously be infringing upon a third party's patent. For such an inventor, the strengths they gain from placing their patent are weaknesses vis-à-vis the third party's patent.

In conclusion, even the rational utilitarian approach may not be sufficient to fully justify the existence of the patent. On the other hand, it offers interesting insight into the dynamics of the patent and the possibility of finding an acceptable balance between the different forces involved.

THE PATENT: A DELICATE BALANCE

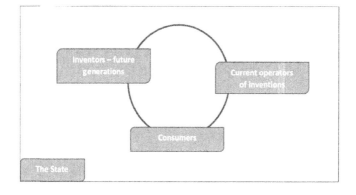

The main stakeholders of the patent

Source: Diagram by the author

STAKEHOLDERS WITH
CONFLICTING INTERESTS

The patent involves a multitude of direct and indirect stakeholders. For the sake of simplicity, we will focus here on the three main players as represented in the diagram above: the current operators of patented inventions, consumers and future generations of inventors. Each of these groups has its own interests, and a utilitarian view of patenting seeks the best possible means of balancing them.

The first group is made up of individuals or companies that exploit an invention, either by manufacturing it or by distributing it commercially. The operators may be the inventors themselves or their successors in title, such as their employers. Their objective is to control the invention so as to generate maximum profit.

The second group is the consumers, i.e. the users of the inventions made available by the operators. The main objective of this group is to have access to the inventions under the best conditions, in particular at the lowest possible price.

Finally, the third group consists of future generations of inventors. In the future, they will take the place of current inventors and their inventions will be deployed by new operators, thus commencing a new cycle. The interest of future inventors is to be able to thoroughly understand the inventions of the present in order to improve them and use them as a basis for future inventions.

It is immediately clear that the objectives pursued by these different types of stakeholders differ substantially and often diverge. For example, the operators' search for maximum profit conflicts with the consumers' search for the lowest price. Likewise, the desire to control inventions does not encourage operators to disclose them to future inventors because they are potential future competitors.

As noted earlier, in the absence of patents, operators would naturally tend to keep their inventions secret where possible in order to avoid the risk of exploitation by others. As long as secrecy can be maintained and competition excluded, operators are in a *de facto* monopoly position that allows them to generate profit. On the other hand, once the secrecy is lifted, for example as a result of a disclosure or an independent discovery by a third party, competition sets in, driving down the selling price of inventions to the benefit of consumers. It is also necessary to wait for the secret to be out for future inventors to be able to learn about the inventions and use them as inspiration for their own developments. This system is inefficient and does not really benefit consumers or, above all, future innovation.

What happens when the patent mechanism is introduced into this system?

Operators can then choose to control their inventions through patent protection, rather than through secrecy. The exclusivity conferred by the patent makes it possible for the operators to offer a unique and attractive product or service, which they can sell at a price higher than the marginal cost – i.e. the cost of producing an extra copy of the invention –

that would be charged in a fully competitive market without patent protection. The extra profit thus generated benefits the operators of the patented inventions to the detriment of consumers (within certain limits, however, since there are, in most cases, alternative offers available to the consumers such that the patent does not confer a true economic monopoly). Moreover, the extra cost charged is likely to result in what economists call a "deadweight loss" to society, as some consumers choose to do without a patented product altogether because they consider it too expensive.

In the case of future inventors, the patent improves the situation considerably. The publication of patents ensures the circulation of technical knowledge and the security provided to the patent holders facilitates technology transfers. Future inventors can therefore conduct their research more efficiently by "standing on the shoulders of giants" of previous generations. In this way, innovation can continue to develop.

Does this mean that consumers would lose the most following the introduction of the patent? This would be too hasty a conclusion. First of all, consumers benefit indirectly, although very concretely, from the innovation fostered by the patent system because it improves social welfare. It is impossible to know with certainty what the world would look like without patents, but it is clear that the patent systems in place have not prevented (and may even have enabled) the development of technologies that have revolutionized, among other things, our ways of communicating (the internet, cell phones, social networks), travelling (high-speed trains, autonomous vehicles, space travel), and healing ourselves (drugs, vaccines, health sciences). If the availability of such technologies to the public can be attributed, at least in part, to patents and their stimulating effect on innovation, this probably more than compensates for the "deadweight loss" mentioned above.

Moreover, consumers are not the only stakeholders who incur costs as a result of the existence of the patent. For example, most of the costs involved in obtaining and defending patents fall upon the patent holders themselves. Many patent offices set their fees in such a way as to ensure a financial balance. However, not all patents are profitable for the operators. Future inventors are not absolute winners either. While they have access to valuable knowledge, they may find themselves blocked by a situation where their improvements are not free to practice because a pre-existing patent is in place. This can happen, for example, when the owners of major prior patents refuse to license them and there is no way around their authority. In such cases, the incentive to innovate for future generations disappears. As a result, each group of stakeholders incurs both benefits and costs due to the existence of patents. The issue cannot therefore be reduced to one of so-called "winners" and "losers" of the system.

On the other hand, it should be noted that the patent has intrinsic characteristics that enable it to limit the costs mentioned above and to thus increase the overall cost/benefit ratio. The limited duration of the patent (presently set at 20 years) is a way of lightening the financial burden on consumers once the patent holder has theoretically been able to make a return on their initial investment. It is also a way to prevent present day operators from charging perpetual rent on inventions, leaving room for the innovators of the future. According to another example, implementing certain criteria for patentability, such as novelty or the inventive step, guarantees against the granting or maintenance of unjustified monopolies on inventions deemed too trivial. This prevents the excessive disruption of existing industries (as could happen in the time of Elizabeth I) and limits blocks in which no one is free to operate – a situation that ultimately harms consumers by depriving them of innovative products on the market.

In light of the above, it is clear that the patent is a matter of compromise which, without fully satisfying each stakeholder, is likely to establish a balance acceptable to most. To achieve this balance, it is necessary that the characteristics of the patent be appropriately regulated. It is apparent that a patent that is designed to be too weak – i.e. a patent that cannot be effectively enforced against third parties, such as a patent with too short a duration – would excessively harm the current operators and risk causing them to move away from the system permanently. On the other hand, a patent that is too strong, such as one with a scope that is too broad to be designed around, would give too much market power to the operators, who could then impose prohibitive sales prices on consumers. The optimal balance therefore lies somewhere between these extreme positions. But where exactly? And how do we get there? This is where another stakeholder comes in: the State.

Currier & Ives
Washington and His Cabinet, 1896

Three members of this cabinet formed
the American Patent Board at the end of the 18th century.

THE STATE: A KEY PLAYER

When looking at the effects of the patent, one must not forget that it is a right granted by a state. In this regard, it is the role of the state to shape its patent system by means of sovereign law. How does the state take on this responsibility?

One might think that, as the representative of civil society, the state looks primarily to protect its citizens, who are all consumers, from the above-mentioned risks of excessive prices and deadweight loss. In such a case, the state would guarantee access to technologies for as many people as possible. At the same time, however, it must also ensure that current operators of inventions have sufficient incentives to bring them to market so that contemporary national industry can thrive. It must also take a long-term view and make room for future innovation, without which the economy would be at risk of freezing sooner or later. In short, the state does not represent any specific category of stakeholder, or rather, it represents them all simultaneously!

The state is therefore a key player in that it introduces a dynamic element into the balance of forces presented above. It has the power to move this balance in one direction or another by favoring one actor over another. On what criteria then does the state base its tuning? As suggested by our brief historical review, the answer to this question is complex and varies according to time and place.

As we have seen, the old royal privileges, for example, underpinned the mercantilist policies of the 16th and 17th centuries, which aimed to develop a self-sufficient local industry. Through these policies, the state particularly favored the operators of new industries, offering them advantageous conditions without imposing on them many obligations. It nevertheless took precautions to preserve a certain balance and protect the interests of other groups of stakeholders, like in the case of Henry Smyth who, in order to obtain a letters patent in 1552, had to accept not to harm citizens or existing industries.

During the French Revolution, movement away from the preliminary examination of inventions modified the pre-existing balance by allowing inventors to obtain patents almost without conditions. One can imagine that consumers and emergent innovators were harmed by this move. One can also appreciate state's embarrassment at being made to enact quite radical change in order to contain the revolutionary surge.

Closer to our time, the alternating strengthening and weakening of patent holders' rights in U.S. law and jurisprudence over the past few decades has produced a pendulum effect. This is another illustration of how states make continuous readjustments to the unstable balance between stakeholders.

These examples show that the state and its institutions tune the parameters of the national patent system so that it is in line with the economic policies of the time. Thus, when it comes to the patent, the state seeks not only to satisfy its citizens, but also to serve what it perceives to be its own interests.

Over time, the state oscillates between two needs that serve the national interests: on one hand, technical development; on the other, the protection of national industry. The first motive involves creating new industries in the country that develop new technologies that improve social welfare. This technical development is likely to lead to economic development and growth. The second need of the state is to strengthen national industries by providing them with means of protection, for example against foreign competition. While the second approach generally follows the first chronologically, with the birth of an industry preceding its consolidation, the two can coexist. A greater weight can be attributed to one or the other depending on the priorities of the state. The patent is precisely one of the tools that is used for this tuning. It acts as a cursor between the two positions mentioned above and gives the state the control it needs to put its economic policy into action.

Thus, a state that perceives itself as being behind technologically has an interest in encouraging technical development in the country, even if that involves copying technologies created abroad without authorization. In terms of patents, this can be achieved by adopting a weak patent system that does not prevent the reproduction of valuable inventions conceived elsewhere or by legalizing counterfeiting to a certain extent. In an extreme case, the state may even decide not to have a patent system at all. This was the choice made by the Netherlands when it abolished its patent system in 1869 in response to a moment of industrial weakness where nearly 90% of Dutch patents were granted to foreign applicants. Even the newly independent United States, which had developed a modern patent system, was careful to discriminate against foreign inventors in order to maintain its capacity to catch up technologically, especially vis-à-vis then flourishing

British industry. In 1919, Great Britain excluded chemicals from the scope of patentability so as to be able to copy and put on the British market the inventions of the powerful German chemical industry without any compensation. After the Second World War, Italy stopped granting patents to pharmaceutical products in order to be able to manufacture drugs invented in the United States in particular. History is full of examples where states deliberately weakened their patent systems, at least in selected technical areas, for the purpose of national development.

Once the imitation strategy has produced effects in the country and enabled it to learn enough to move from being a copier to an innovator, keeping the patent system too weak would be counterproductive as it would prevent new domestic innovators from thriving. A strengthening of the patent system then becomes necessary to reward and support these innovators by protecting them from being copied by infringers who have not invested in the country's technical development in the same way.

Obviously, the patent is only one tool among others to implement the economic policy of a country. For example, nowadays, many countries put innovation at the core of their development strategy. To this end, they have a range of instruments available, such as the orientation of public research towards certain identified technical fields or the public sponsorship of private players by means of targeted subsidies. Nonetheless, the patent is certainly different from other tools in that it can be adjusted according to the current needs. Whether it is weakened or strengthened, it is indeed capable of fulfilling very different, even opposing, objectives without ever completely breaking the balance between stakeholders in a way that would excessively harm one of them. The patent thus represents an especially attractive tool of dynamic control for the state and its institutions.

It should be noted, however, that this analysis is valid in the case of a state that is isolated from the rest of the world. As we have seen previously, recent history has led many countries to harmonize their patent laws as part of binding international treaties. The ability of a state to change its legislation or even its patent practice in a way that does not comply with international agreements is thus reduced in the present day.

Similarly, despite the flexibility it offers, the patent should not be considered a dependable tool with totally predictable consequences. Indeed, experience shows that the many changes made over time to strengthen or weaken patent systems (e.g. by modifying the terms of protection, the patentability criteria, the ease of invalidating a patent, the ease of obtaining injunctive relief against an infringer, etc.) have not always produced the effects expected by the experts. The number of patent filings, grants, litigation cases or transactions does not seem to vary in correlation with these changes. This is the interesting phenomenon observed by law Professor Mark A. Lemley, which he calls "the surprising resilience of the patent system". One hypothesis to explain this phenomenon is that patent stakeholders have their own agendas that are unrelated to the specific characteristics of patents. Initiating a patent infringement action may be justified, for example, by commercial considerations or by the ego of decision-makers, which have little to do with patent law but find in the patent a useful tool to achieve their goals. The level of control by the state therefore ends where the strategic behavior of the users of the patent system begins.

Whatever balance it achieves with the patent, the state is generally mindful of encouraging innovation in the country. However, assuming that the patent, strong or weak, is really capable of meeting this goal, is it the best tool to do so?

THE BEST TOOL FOR INNOVATION

A.D. 1769 . . . . N° 913.

Steam Engines, &c.

WATT'S SPECIFICATION.

TO ALL TO WHOM THESE PRESENTS SHALL COME, I, James Watt, of Glasgow, in Scotland, Merchant, send greeting.

WHEREAS His most Excellent Majesty King George the Third, by His Letters Patent under the Great Seal of Great Britain, bearing date the Fifth
5 day of January, in the ninth year of His said Majesty's reign, did give and grant unto me, the said James Watt, His special licence, full power, sole priviledge and authority, that I, the said James Watt, my exors, adñors, and assigns, should and lawfully might, during the term of years therein expressed, use, exercise, and vend, throughout that part of His Majesty's
10 Kingdom of Great Britain called England, the Dominion of Wales, and Town of Berwick upon Tweed, and also in His Majesty's Colonies and Plantations abroad, my " NEW INVENTED METHOD OF LESSENING THE CONSUMPTION OF STEAM AND FUEL IN FIRE ENGINES;" in which said recited Letters Patent is contained a proviso obliging me, the said James Watt, by writing under my hand and seal, to
15 cause a particular description of the nature of the said Invention to be inrolled in His Majesties High Court of Chancery within four calendar months after the date of the said recited Letters Patent, as in and by the said Letters Patent, and the Statute in that behalf made, relation being thereunto respectively had, may more at large appear.
20 NOW KNOW YE, that in compliance with the said provisoe, and in pursuance of the said Statute, I, the said James Watt, do hereby declare that the

The first English patent granted to James Watt

Dated 1769, it relates to a steam engine
with a separate condensation chamber.

DOES THE PATENT REALLY ENCOURAGE INNOVATION?

Does the patent really encourage innovation? This question has haunted economists for decades. Put another way, this question asks whether the incentive that patents offer to present innovators (by making them hope for a return on their investments) outweighs the cost they impose on future generations of inventors (whose innovation programs may be aborted to avoid infringing earlier patents).

This question is important because encouraging innovation is one of the main modern justifications for patents. If the answer were negative, it would undermine the idea that patents are one of the progressive factors that, among other successes, led to the first industrial revolution in England in the 19th century (think, for example, of James Watt's patented steam engine, which improved Thomas Newcomen's steam pump and caused industry to take off), as well as to the technological emergence and then dominance of the United States in the 20th century.

In fact, the answer to this question is far from binary. As early as 1958, the Austrian economist Fritz Machlup famously stated that, according to the knowledge of the time, it would be irresponsible to introduce a patent system if one did not already exist, but it would be equally irresponsible to abolish the system that was already in place. Surprising as it may seem, the many studies conducted since Machlup have not reached a definitive conclusion as to the actual effectiveness of patents in accelerating innovation. This uncertainty has unfortunately created room for ideological bias and unnuanced positions.

Despite this fuzziness, some factual elements can nevertheless be established. First of all, patents seem to be more effective in some fields than in others. This is the case in the pharmaceutical field, where the investments to be made in the early stages of product development are particularly significant (it is not unusual for the cost of developing a drug to exceed a billion U.S. dollars), technical progress is fairly slow (a drug can remain on the market for many decades) and the final product can be described in a relatively unequivocal manner (some drugs are entirely characterized by a single molecule). In such a case, the hope of profitability offered by the patent represents a strong incentive to move forward with investment. On the other hand, in technical fields such as in computer science and telecommunications, these conditions are not met. Since initial investments are relatively low, innovation occurs at a rapid pace and inventions are characterized by a plurality of features, the incentive offered by the patent is smaller in these fields. While adjusting the characteristics of the patent according to the field in which it is made could solve this difficulty, doing so would open the door to complex debates on the specificities of each field and undermine the simplicity of the system.

Nowadays, the generalization and harmonization of patent systems around the world have made it impossible to conduct comparative studies on whether a country's success in innovation can be explained by patents. We must therefore look back to the past to find answers. In this respect, the fascinating research of Petra Moser is very helpful. This economist has studied data on thousands of innovations presented at the World Fairs of 1851 and 1876 – a period when not all countries had patent systems and those in existence varied widely from one location to another.

Moser's work reveals that innovation was lively in countries without patents, sometimes even more so than in countries with patents. Switzerland and Denmark, two countries without patents at the time, contributed twice as many exhibits per capita compared with other European countries in 1851. Moreover, their exhibited innovations were of at least equal quality to those of countries with patent systems, as evidenced by the large number of prizes they won for ingenuity and utility. These data suggest that patents do not have a significant effect on the *volume* and *quality* of innovation. However, we cannot leave it at that.

The influence of patents on innovation is real, but it is most apparent in shaping the *direction* of innovation. Petra Moser has shown that the innovations exhibited by countries without patents, albeit numerous, were limited to a small set of industries, such as scientific instruments, chemistry, textile dyes and food products. What the products of these industries had in common in the mid-nineteenth century was that they were not easily reverse engineered. That is to say they could not be analyzed in a way that would allow anyone to reproduce them. As such, these products were sufficiently well protected by secrecy. By contrast, the innovations exhibited by countries with patent systems appeared in a much broader set of industries, such as mechanical engineering and agriculture. Among the patent system countries, such as Great Britain and the United States, only a small fraction of the inventions exhibited were patented, and they belonged to the same industrial fields. It follows that innovators tend to focus on certain technical areas based on the protection they provide over inventions. While fields where secrecy offers a satisfactory level of protection are exploited by all, areas where secrecy is ineffective are exploited only by innovators in patent system countries. In other words, the patent makes innovation possible in all technical fields, including those that are not attractive *a priori* because they do not offer natural protection through secrecy.

Is this theory confirmed by other historical data? To find out, we need to go back to the Netherlands and Switzerland at the end of the 19th century and the beginning of the 20th century. As you will recall, the former abolished their patent system in 1869 before reinstating it in 1912, while the latter deferred the adoption of its own system until 1888. These fairly recent events provide us with relevant comparison points on the innovation that exists in a country depending on whether or not it has a patent system.

We have seen above that the Netherlands was not particularly oriented towards industrial innovation during this time. The number of patents filed before the abolition of the system was low and a large majority of them were granted to foreigners. Despite a period of more than four decades without patents, the situation had not fundamentally changed by the time the Dutch patent system was reintroduced in 1912. Neither the abolition nor the reintroduction of patents seems to have had any significant effect on the country's distant relationship with innovation. However, the abolition of patents in 1869 was followed by a significant increase in the share of innovations in fields that were not very dependent on patents, such as food products.

Unlike the Netherlands, Switzerland in the second half of the 19th century was extremely innovative. However, innovation was concentrated among a limited set of products, such as watches, music boxes, chocolate and foods. In these craft industries, where know-how was essential, secrecy provided adequate protection. Things started to change, however, when mechanization entered these domains, causing Switzerland to lose some of its advantages to large industrialized countries such as the United States. Secrecy became insufficient to protect the interests of Swiss manufacturers, so the introduction of patent protection became a necessity in 1888. After the Swiss patent system was introduced, innovation boomed in the country (which is indirectly shown by the sharp increase in the number of U.S. patents filed by Swiss inventors before and after 1888). This innovation spread into many new technical fields, such as textiles, dyes, lighting and turbines. At the same time, innovation in Switzerland's traditional fields of excellence slowed down considerably.

The examples of the Netherlands and Switzerland thus seem to confirm that although patents alone cannot influence the quantity of innovation, they have an obvious multiplying effect on the directions taken by innovation because they enable its growth in industrial fields that would not be attractive in the absence of patents. Hence, patents "unlock" an abundance of innovation.

This conclusion is all the more important since the fields where secrecy confers sufficient protection tend to shrink over time as technology evolves. As scientific knowledge advances and analytical methods become more powerful, a decreasing number of inventions are still capable of effectively resisting reverse engineering efforts that would reveal trade secrets. For example, Mendeleev's publication of the periodic table of elements in 1869 facilitated chemical analysis, making the protection of a chemical composition by secrecy too weak. At a time when many inventions find their expression in a computer program and the theft of computer data is spreading, secrecy as a tool to protect against the copying of technical inventions could become even less effective in the future. The patent offers an effective solution in a context where secrecy could be less and less relevant, at least in certain fields.

Given the impact of patents on the direction of innovation, governments should set their patent systems in line with the technological orientation and economic policy they choose. However, they should show restraint and refrain from excessively strengthening their patents. This would help them to avoid favoring too much the operators of the present to the detriment of future innovation, as the latter represents the only way to ensure sustainable and responsible growth.

While the properly used patent has a beneficial effect on the direction of innovation, is there not a better alternative, capable of encouraging innovation in all its dimensions?

Swedish patent application by Alfred Nobel
on the principles of ignition of nitroglycerin,
the origin of dynamite, 1864

What are the alternatives to the patent?

According to the utilitarian approach mentioned above, the patent cannot fully satisfy all the stakeholders at the same time and can only offer a compromise situation. The question follows: might there be a more optimal solution, one that meets every stakeholder's ideal? In order to do so, we will examine some alternatives to the patent.

The first alternative that comes to mind is to offer no legal protection at all for inventions. Thus, inventors can choose whether or not to invest time and effort in developing a technique and making it available to the public at their own cost and without being able to count on any compensation. Because of the informational nature of inventions outlined above, inventors would then lack the incentive to innovate. Some may be satisfied with such a situation and be happy to work for the common good rather than for their own financial interest. This was the case for inventors such as Benjamin Franklin, already mentioned above, or Alexander Fleming. The latter, a British physician and biologist, discovered by accident in 1928 that a mold called penicillin had the ability to kill bacteria. By isolating penicillin, Fleming paved the way for the treatment of bacterial infections with antibiotics, for which he was awarded the Nobel Prize in Medicine in 1945, along with Howard Florey and Ernst Chain. Fleming, aware as he was that clinical use of penicillin could save lives, chose not to patent it for ethical reasons. However, such a model of selfless sharing does not sit well with our current way of life; it is not surprising that only a few exceptional inventors are ready to follow it. For most inventors and operators of inventions, the lack of incentive resulting from a lack of protection would instead discourage them from investing in innovation, which would ultimately deprive society of innovative products.

If they nevertheless decided to pursue innovation, inventors and invention operators would logically put in place strategies aimed at still making some profit from their work. For example, they might try to be first on the market and/or take control of assets complementary to the invention so as to obtain a commercial advantage over their competitors. However, this advantage is fragile and ephemeral; a more powerful competitor, even one that is late to the market, can always copy the innovation and possibly attract the majority of customers. Therefore, in the absence of legal protection for the inventor, the law of the strongest may well apply.

Another way for inventors to earn some income from their inventions in the absence of legal protection would be to keep them secret. This option seems to be quite natural, as evidenced by the authoritarian and innovation-averse practice of the old guilds described in the first part of this book. This was indeed the approach that preceded the granting of royal privileges and the issuance of the first patents. To a certain extent, it has also survived the advent of the latter, as secrecy is still widely used today, often as a complement to patents. As already mentioned, however, secrecy is not sufficient on its own, as it can be extinguished as soon as the same invention is made independently by a third party. Furthermore, some inventions are impossible to protect by secrecy because their characteristics are detectable with the naked eye or from a reverse engineering analysis. This explains why innovation based on secrecy only develops in a set of technical fields much narrower than those supported by patents.

Whether total open-source transparency or systematic secrecy are in place, the absence of a specific right over inventions thus seems to lead to a dead end that proves harmful to the development of innovation. It remains to be seen whether there are other types of incentives that could replace patents in an advantageous way.

One solution is to award inventors a prize (i.e. a financial reward) for their contribution to resolving a given problem. This idea is not new; traces of it can be found in the old royal privileges, which were granted in a discretionary way in exchange for a favor done to the state. It was recently revived by the Nobel Prize-winning economist Joseph Stiglitz. He considers prizes to be better than patents for incentivizing innovative work that is not compatible with a market economy – work unlikely to be commercially successful, such as the development of drugs for rare orphan diseases or health issues that mainly affect disadvantaged countries. In this vision, prizes would cover the cost of research, meaning that inventors or operators would not have to worry about making their investments profitable in the long term and that the cost of profit-making would not have to be passed on to the final consumers.

The prize tool is sometimes used in the private sphere, where companies use it to trigger and benefit from innovations coming from outside. For example, Netflix used it in 2009 to improve its algorithm for predicting user ratings of content. At the end of a competition, an award of one million dollars was given to a team that was able to outperform Netflix's original algorithm. But would the generalization of this mechanism under the control of the state be more efficient and equitable than the patent system?

The economist B. Zorina Khan has devoted much of her research to this question. Her answer is clear: no. Indeed, unlike patented inventions, whose success depends on the self-regulating laws of the market, the awarding of prizes requires an autonomous infrastructure to judge the value of inventions. This model leads to a situation of monopsony (the mirror image of monopoly), where a single buyer is able to choose among several suppliers of technical solutions. The selection made by the buyer can be based on their own criteria, which are not necessarily connected to the needs of the market and are not required to be totally transparent. As in the days of privileges, there is therefore a great risk that the choice be based on arbitrary, subjective, biased or even discriminatory criteria. Unlike patents, the validity of which can be challenged before an independent court of law, an effective challenge to prize awards seems less feasible.

In addition, awarding prizes is based on a very high degree of selectivity, since only a few solutions are selected from a potentially much larger number of submissions. The winning solution eliminates all others, leaving very little chance for most disqualified innovations to reach the market. Furthermore, the winner themself may feel frustrated when the amount received from the prize is far below the revenue that the placement of a patent could have generated.

Finally, by design, the awarding of prizes orients research as the participants all attempt to solve the same technical problem selected by the competition organizer. This can be an advantage when one wishes to channel innovation in specific directions poorly served by the market. At the same time, however, researchers lose a part of their freedom to solve the problem of their choice.

This loss of opportunity would imply a drying up of innovation in directions not targeted by the prizes.

Prizes are therefore not free of problems. If one follows the convincing theory of B. Zorina Khan, their effectiveness would be much lesser than that of patents, especially for the development of innovation. Other mechanisms of direct or indirect financing of innovation by the state are conceivable, but they would likely suffer from the same weaknesses as prizes.

In conclusion, the known alternative solutions do not appear to be clearly superior to patents. This observation – combined with the fact that the transition from a patent system to an alternative system alone would incur a high cost – certainly explains why there is no historical precedent for a permanent shift away from patents to another system. On the contrary, all countries have eventually adopted a patent system. This does not mean, however, that patents should exclude any other adequate means to encourage innovation. Optimal efficiency can probably be achieved in the appropriate combined use of patents, secrecy and public financing of innovation.

If the patent has stood the test of time so well, it is not only because of its superiority over alternative systems, but also because of its capacity to reinvent itself constantly. New uses of the patent regularly come up – uses and practices that the inventors of the past could probably never have imagined.

NEW USES AND PRACTICES

Quadricycle Peugeot, 1893

This is one of the first gasoline-powered vehicles.
It can drive at 20 km/h. Its wheels are equipped with a rubber sheath.

Source: Picture taken by the author at the Arts et Métiers Museum, Paris, 2021

A TOOL TO SUPPORT
THE BUSINESS STRATEGY OF COMPANIES

The inventive act comes from the human brain. It is therefore logical that the inventor should be perceived as the key player and natural owner of their invention. However, an inventor is not necessarily an entrepreneur, as these two functions require very different skills. Even if they have all the required skills, an inventor rarely has the necessary resources, most notably financial, to exploit their invention. This is especially true in industrial fields that call for major investments, in order to provide equipment and qualified staff, for instance. Moreover, in the most complex fields, the range of technical knowledge required is such that only multidisciplinary teams can make valuable inventions. For these reasons, an isolated inventor is often not best placed to transform their invention into a successful innovation. This explains why another type of legal person has progressively taken control of innovation: companies.

In the past, it was already not uncommon for an inventor to join forces with one or more business executives to help them manufacture and market their invention.

Companies combine these technical and commercial profiles within the same organization, making it possible to go further since the different players of innovation all serve a common business strategy. The inventor thus becomes a mere employee whose inventions are appropriated by the company for which they work.

During the 20th century, companies only used their patents marginally and for primarily defensive purposes. It was only in the 1980s that they started to use them in a much more strategic way. This change is related to the fact that the share of intangible assets in the value of companies has been growing steadily over time. While they represented barely 17% of the value of companies in 1975, intangible assets comprised 90% of their value in 2020 according to a study by Ocean Tomo. In technology companies, patents make up a large part of these prized assets. It is therefore important to protect them and exploit their full value.

In addition to their traditional functions of excluding unauthorized third parties and selecting licensees who will be able to exploit an invention in exchange for the payment of royalties, patents now play a multitude of other, alternative or complementary roles within companies. Some of these roles operate the level of company-employee relations. For example, patents may serve as a means for the company to appropriate the knowledge of its employees, to support the granting of additional remunerations to reward the merit of inventive employees, and to stimulate the creativity of the employees.

The patent also plays a role in the company's relations with third parties and with competitors in particular. In this way, a published patent can be used by the company to signal their presence or expertise in a given field. The company can also use it to dissuade third parties from competing within its private preserve. On the contrary, when a competitor has already claimed a field with its own patents, a company can use its patent portfolio as leverage to reach an agreement that allows each party to exercise its activity peacefully (for example, by means of cross-licenses whereby each party licenses its patents to the other).

As can be seen from these examples, the patent can be used in many ways depending on what a company's intentions. Various strategies can be adopted according to the objective at hand. For example, a company producing and marketing a highly differentiating technical solution may opt for a strategy of systematic exclusion of third parties in order to preserve its originality, while another company with limited financial resources may choose to license out its patents to as many parties as possible in order to generate maximum revenue. In this respect, there is no absolute optimal strategy; the best strategy, for a given company, is the one that will enable it to best achieve its own objectives. This multiplicity of roles and the ability to adapt to various strategies afforded by the plasticity of the patent represent considerable assets for companies that know how to use them. At the same time, they introduce complexities that make it difficult for observers to analyze the effects of patents macroscopically. This is one of the sources of misunderstanding and distrust of patents.

This distrust has grown in recent years alongside abusive behavior on the part of certain patent holders. Indeed, the exclusive right offered by the patent was originally conceived as a means for the patent holder to exist. Without this legal protection, a new entrant would have no space to thrive in a competitive environment where the established players could freely copy its inventions. However, powerful players in a market may tend to use patents as insurmountable barriers for new entrants. By repeatedly filing patents on multiple aspects of a technical solution and aggressively enforcing them, such patent holders have sometimes been able to create excessive monopolies, thereby severely reducing competition in the long run. As economist Philippe Aghion puts it, in order to preserve their assets and not become victims of creative destruction themselves, these market players have transformed their innovation rent into a situation rent, killing competition and leading to an overall loss of economic efficiency.

It should be noted, however, that there are forces in place to limit and sanction such abuses. The first one is to be found in competition and anti-trust laws. Although patents inherently distort competition, they cannot go beyond what competition law allows. Even if they own patents, companies are not allowed to abuse their dominant position. Put simply, patents cannot be used as a pretext to excessively crush competition.

The second force likely to counteract some companies' desire to dominate is to be found in society itself. Companies are increasingly adopting the view that they bear a social responsibility. Although they are not, strictly speaking, accountable to society, they are increasingly attentive to the sensibilities of the public. This public pressure can be sufficient, in some cases, to prevent abuses of patents without the law or the state having to intervene.

In this respect, it is noteworthy that younger generations seem to be developing a more acute awareness of the individual responsibility of each person towards contemporary society and future generations. Companies are now built around societal projects and ethical values that go beyond the mere search for profit. One can hope that the patent will favorably support this evolution, as it has been able to support all company strategies until now. For example, one can imagine that a socially responsible company could decide to assign its patents and license them out only to players that share its values.

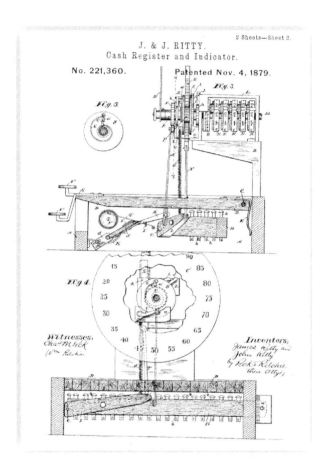

U.S. patent granted in 1879 to the brothers James and John Ritty,
the inventors of the first cash register

With this cash register, James, who owned a saloon in Ohio,
wanted to prevent the theft of revenues by his employees.

A TOOL FOR MONETIZATION

Obtaining and enforcing a patent comes at a cost. If an inventor or their successor in title chooses to incur the corresponding cost, it is because they hope for a direct or indirect return on their investment. The value of a patent is, however, difficult to estimate. This is due first of all to a lack of relevant reference points. (Strictly speaking, there is not one organized market for patents, and even if there are numerous transactions, their financial details are not always known and the situations are not always comparable.) Secondly, the value of a patent can only be relative: the same patent may have a low value in the hands of a company that does not have the means to exploit it, or a high value when it is held, for instance, by a company that holds complementary assets. To compensate for the costs incurred and generate a maximum income, the owner of a patent is therefore naturally tempted to monetize it.

Very early on, inventors sought to propose their technologies to interested third parties capable of exploiting them by offering that they pay for licenses on their patents. Samuel Hopkins, the inventor who obtained the very first U.S. patent in 1790 for his potash manufacturing process, is a good example of this reality. Hopkins spent a great deal of time and energy promoting his invention and enlisted the help of his son-in-law and lawyers to license out his patent. This trend took off in the 19th century, when companies were created (in the case of Thomas Edison, for example) with the sole purpose of undertaking research. Such research endeavors were financed by license royalties, leaving it to industrial manufacturers to produce their inventions. This model reflects the efficiency resulting from the separation of the functions of inventing, on the one hand, and marketing, on the other. By specializing in research, inventors become more prolific and come up with better quality inventions. Similarly, industrial players are better placed than inventors to ensure the commercial success of their inventions.

This phenomenon was called into question during the Second World War, during which industrial players, particularly in the U.S., received large amounts of public funding to design and produce technologies likely to procure an advantage over the enemy. In-house research and development laboratories therefore appeared and remained in operation after the war. The model then ran out of steam at the end of the 20th century, its results proving inconclusive. For example, in 1996, the telecommunications company AT&T separated from its "Bell Labs".

The separation of functions and the specialization of players have gained new momentum in recent years as technology has invaded the public space. There are now countless start-ups and other small-scale structures whose added value lies entirely in technology. These companies often have neither the capacity nor the desire to become full-fledged manufacturers, preferring instead to offer their services or sell their technology to larger companies that already have the necessary infrastructure to manufacture products and distribute them to consumers. On their end, these larger companies benefit from effective external research and development without having to bear the costs, especially in the event of failure. By accessing the technology of a start-up through agreements of various types (licenses, partnerships, investments, acquisitions, etc.), they can launch quality products on the market in very short time. In most agreements, patents play a key role in securing such technology transfer.

While patent licenses may seem as old as the patents themselves, they are not all equal. In recent years, *non-practicing entities* (NPEs) have multiplied. These entities often have no other activity than licensing patents. Some NPEs act as intermediaries on behalf of inventors or their successors in title. Others act on their own behalf and purchase patents from companies that are bankrupt or have lost interest in the protected technology.

The abusive practices of some NPEs have earned them the label of "*patent trolls*" and a less than friendly characterization. Among these practices, one can note a high degree of aggression; trolls reach out to a very large number of companies implementing their patents (sometimes incidentally and often unknowingly) and threaten them with swift legal action if they refuse to adopt a license on almost non-negotiable terms. Such an action puts the targeted companies at risk of incurring high defense costs and, if the judge grants an injunction, of having to stop their business activity. For small operating companies with limited means to defend themselves, the threat can be existential, forcing them to accept the set terms at any cost. Some trolls use other tactics to artificially increase the amount of royalties due by, for example, first concealing themselves through complex legal arrangements and then revealing themselves at a time when the operating companies have already incurred sunken costs and are in a very weak position to negotiate the terms of the license. This business model is relatively low risk for NPEs; since they have no industrial activity, they cannot be subject to the threat of a patent infringement counteraction from their targets.

Some observers take the position that the above-mentioned negative narrative is irrelevant and that patent trolls are not really different from other licensors. However, I believe that the activity of trolls is at odds with the philosophy of patents because it inverts several of their usual characteristics. First of all, trolls do not regard patent infringement as a nuisance that should be stopped in order to restore the owner's exclusive right to exploit their invention or not. Instead, they see such infringements as opportunities for financial gain; the more infringers there are and the more widespread the infringement, the higher the gain expected by trolls. In addition, trolls distort the traditional notion of the license. Rather than providing an opportunity to a licensee wishing to develop their activity through the patented technique, licenses "offered" under duress by trolls do not confer any other benefit than the possibility of continuing a current business activity. Such a license is therefore a "stick" without any "carrot" dimension; there is no reward at stake. Finally, contrary to the underlying idea of the patent system according to which exclusivity rewards intellectual work and compensates for the investments made at the outset, the benefits sought by trolls are disconnected from these considerations, if not totally arbitrary. They are limited only by what the targeted companies are willing to pay to get rid of the threat, which can far exceed the real value of the patents at hand. The capacity of trolls to monetize patents is almost unlimited when infringement is widespread.

Contrary to what some claim, the activity of trolls does not benefit innovation because, in most cases, the original inventors do not gain any profit from subsequent transactions. On the other hand, the threats made to operating companies are likely to destabilize them, inflicting possible negative outcomes on their production and innovation.

It has been argued that patent trolls are not a new phenomenon. The first troll in history may be the American inventor Elias Howe, holder of the U.S. patent 4750 made in 1846 and relating to an improvement made to sewing machines. Howe did not use his invention but, taking advantage of the broad scope of his patent, threatened the major sewing machine operators of the time with infringement actions. The royalties he required to license out his technology were $25 per machine, a very substantial amount considering the price of a machine back then (about one fifth of the retail cost). Within 15 years, Howe made a fortune from this business model.

This example certainly shows that patent trolls have existed in the past. Nonetheless, it should not erase the fact that the phenomenon has exploded in the 21st century. Every year since 2008, the majority of defendants in infringement actions in the United States have been sued by NPEs rather than by operating companies, despite the adoption of various measures to limit this trend.

However, not all NPEs are necessarily patent trolls, as defined above. Indeed, by nature, some patent holders do not intend to commercially exploit their inventions. This is the case in universities and research institutes, for example. Generating licensing revenues guarantees that they will be able to continue their research activity, meaning that they cannot be blamed for wanting to monetize their patents. To a certain extent, the same is true for the many industrial companies that do not implement all of their patents for various reasons. Yet, even when their motives are not purely speculative, some of these NPEs occasionally engage in the same abusive behavior as trolls. In light of these examples, it is clear that the notion of patent troll is somewhat vague. It can therefore be difficult to make a relevant distinction between different types of NPE, particularly in the law. It is thus probably up to the courts to analyze the facts on a case-by-case basis and to exercise discretion so as not to impede "legitimate" licensing programs, while at the same time sanctioning abuses that are detrimental to innovation.

Licensing is, however, only one way of monetizing patents. The growing importance of patents in our economy has whetted the appetites of various players eager to capture a share of their value. New practices and professions have emerged as awareness of the financial potential of patents has grown. For example, venture capitalists are now investing in promising young technology companies, hoping to recoup and exceed their initial investment when these companies are sold or go public. The existence and quality of a patent portfolio are among the criteria that matter when deciding whether to invest in these companies. Similarly, banks lend funds to start-ups all the more easily if the latter have relevant patents that can be used as collateral. Insurance companies are now willing to cover the costs of some patent disputes, hoping to make a profit from the damages that will be awarded if infringement is confirmed by the court. These are only a few examples, and one can bet that new practices will continue to emerge in the future to extract even more value from patents.

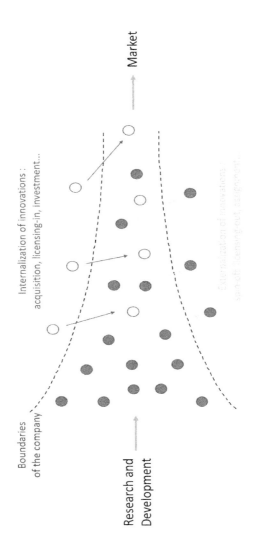

The open innovation model,
based on the work of Henry Chesbrough

Source: Diagram by the author

AN ACCELERATOR FOR COOPERATION

Among the many evolutions and revolutions that the patent has undergone over the centuries is a recent one that has not attracted much attention. Nonetheless, its impact on our economy is strong. This development is known as "open innovation" and relates to the ability of several distinct entities to cooperate in innovation. If this phenomenon amounts to a small revolution, it is because it contradicts the notion that we generally have of patents as tools for appropriation for private purposes and means for the exclusion of third parties. How could patents support exchanges with the outside world?

Yet this is the trend that emerged at the end of the 20th century and the beginning of the 21st century as companies realized that they were not always in the best position to design, develop or market an innovation. Sometimes there are more relevant ideas and more effective means available elsewhere. Not using this external reservoir can be risky for companies, as it can lead them to produce mediocre innovation or, in the worst case, to be overtaken or "disrupted" by other players, sometimes from distant fields. Innovation is not, in fact, a simple matter of will. It cannot be decreed, but must be developed patiently, using various assets including technical skills, commercial skills, production capacities and distribution networks. However, a given company rarely has all the necessary assets to achieve an optimal result.

In this context, Professor Henry Chesbrough formalized the concept of "open innovation" whereby in order to improve their results, companies must also know how to think "externally", using ideas developed elsewhere and taking indirect paths to market when this proves advantageous. This concept is actually quite broad. As shown in the diagram above, it covers a variety of situations, some of which are conventional while others are more innovative. For example, the licensing-in of a patent by a company is an established practice, as mentioned in the previous chapter. On the other hand, the case of a large operating company sharing some of its knowledge and technologies with a third company, as part of a licensing-out agreement or an assignment, is a less conventional situation. The same applies when a company allows some of its employees to take research results away with them and set up their own "spin-off" businesses. Of course, these strategies are not without interest for the companies that use them; they still expect to benefit, for instance by generating revenue from a technology that they would not have been able to implement effectively themselves, or by creating prospects for cooperation with trusted third parties.

Another original characteristic of open innovation is that it does not take place at one a specific stage of innovation but can occur at any point from the design phase to the market launch. At the design stage, for example, a company may choose to work with an external partner to co-develop a technical solution. At the production stage, a start-up may choose to license out its technology or to partner with a larger company that is better positioned to handle large-scale manufacturing.

The cooperation made possible by open innovation can take place between two players only. In other cases, a multiplicity of parties may be involved spanning public and private spheres (e.g. universities licensing their technologies to businesses). Like other approaches, open innovation is capable of using a peer production mode. This is the case with "*crowdsourcing*", for example, where a company faced with a technical problem calls for anyone to participate by proposing their solution and then freely selects the best submission. Using collective intelligence in this way can lead to much better solutions than the one the company would have designed by itself and at a low cost, especially when the problem to be solved belongs to a technical field outside its area of operation.

In one particular case, open innovation projects can be carried out by competitors that nevertheless have an interest in cooperating on a given subject. This is a situation of "co-opetition", where a cooperation project co-exists with a competition relationship. Thus, while clearing the way for new opportunities, open innovation blurs traditional boundaries and makes relationships between players more complex. More and more cases arise where two companies are alternatively or simultaneously in a situation of competition, cooperation, dependence and/or complementarity, depending on the context.

The emergence of this trend may come as a surprise, since there is an inherent risk in sharing information and processes with third parties. Doesn't a company that accepts to share some of its knowledge with the outside world take considerable risk by providing third parties with the means to compete and perhaps ultimately make it obsolete? Why do more and more companies consider this risk to be less than the benefit expected from open innovation?

The answer is to be found in the realm of law. Open innovation projects are covered by legal agreements that protect the parties against unauthorized use of their knowledge. However, these agreements alone are not enough to reassure the parties about the risks of abuse by their partner. Indeed, once information is shared with a third party, it becomes difficult to ensure its control and traceability, despite all possible contractual precautions. What really facilitates peace and trust between the parties is intellectual property law. In the technical field, the legal protection offered by a patent is what can convince its holder to risk disclosing their invention. The patent effectively amounts to a property title which guarantees the origin of the knowledge and can put an end to disallowed uses. Thanks to the patent, the partner is encouraged not to go beyond their contractual rights in order to avoid being charged with infringement. Therefore, paradoxically, it is by erecting fences that exchange between private sectors can be encouraged. By specifying the scope of the protection claimed, the patent secures knowledge transfer and fosters cooperation.

Once again, the patent has shown its capacity to adapt to the needs of the time, as well as a surprising plasticity that allows it to offer a whole range of possibilities, from strict appropriation to a very high level of openness based on cooperation. Total openness is even made possible by the so-called "*patent pledge*", whereby companies keep their patents but publicly declare that they will not enforce their exclusive rights. This mechanism has been used by the car manufacturer Tesla, for example, to promote adoption of its electric vehicle model. Between strict appropriation and patent pledge strategies, companies can find the degree of openness that best suits their aspirations.

Although the patent has been able to adapt effectively until now by developing new uses, it is currently facing huge challenges. What are these new challenges, and can they be overcome?

NEW CHALLENGES AHEAD

U.S. patent 1647 granted to Samuel Morse in 1840
for a new mode of communication of information
via a telegraph – the origin of Morse code

It is allegedly the first software patent in history.

Source: Espacenet - Public domain

Technological challenges

The patent in the face of the fourth Industrial Revolution

By construction, the patent accompanies technical progress. It is therefore not surprising that it has followed and supported great technological milestones in history. As we have seen, the British patent system may have been one of the factors which led to the first Industrial Revolution – that of the steam engine – at the end of the 18th century. The same may have been true in the rest of Europe and in the United States between the end of the 19th and the beginning of the 20th century with the control of oil and electricity, which some consider to mark the second Industrial Revolution.

The rise of computers and telecommunications at the end of the 20th century caused a shock wave for the patent, the effects of which are still being felt today. This third Industrial Revolution has indeed brought about profound economic and social transformations. Software gradually took control over hardware, making automation possible in almost all fields.

From a legal standpoint, the question quickly arose as to how software should be handled given that is an unusual object that seems closer to a work of the mind than to an industrial device. Should it be protected by copyright (as original creative content), by patent (despite its abstract nature), or by both? These questions gave rise to hesitation and controversy. In the United States, it was decided as early as 1983 that the Copyright Act would cover software through the same mechanism applied to literary works. Likewise, copyright has protected the expression of computer programs in France since 1985.

On the side of patents, the situation is not as clear. U.S. law excludes abstract ideas from patentability. As for the European Patent Convention, it expressly states that computer programs, as such, are not considered inventions. Yet many U.S. and European patents are issued every day for computer-implemented inventions. This is understandable given that software is now everywhere and in all industries. Excluding software from patentability would therefore amount to accepting a lack of protection for a large part of today's innovation. To avoid this, the European Patent Office has developed over time a fairly clear and clever case law that recognizes the patentability of computer-implemented inventions, provided that they achieve a so-called additional technical effect. (This case law is known as the "*Comvik* approach", named after the patent holder involved in setting this precedent). In the United States, where the *Diamond v. Diehr* Supreme Court decision opened the door to the patentability of software as early as 1981, the situation has constantly fluctuated between liberal positions (going so far as to protect software for pure financial methods) and restrictive positions (see the *Bilski* and *Alice* decisions, according to which the use of a computer is not sufficient to make an abstract idea patentable). Today, confusion dominates the U.S. context and requests for clarification are becoming more widely expressed from all sides.

In addition, the question of software patentability has become an ideological issue as the concept of "open-source" software has developed. The open-source software model aims to facilitate the use and duplication of software. While there are several variants of the model, which impose greater or fewer obligations on software users, the general idea is to guarantee a certain freedom of use. For the proponents of this model, patents on inventions implemented by software go against their ideals by reintroducing restrictions on use. This is why they argue for the exclusion of software from patentability. Of course, this position conflicts with that of industry stakeholders who want to protect their developments against copying.

The dematerialization of processes has caused tensions in patent systems that were designed at a time when every invention was contained in a concrete machine. Furthermore, the decentralization of technical means, made possible by the advent of telecommunications, has posed new challenges for patents. For example, when the implementation of the steps of a patented process is distributed among a plurality of systems belonging to different persons and located in several countries, how can one determine whether, by whom and under which national law a potential infringement has occurred?

In this context of decentralization, a particularly interesting issue has arisen. Indeed, the distribution of technical means between several devices possibly owned by different manufacturers (for example, a central server, distributed communication relays and the cell phone of an end user) requires interoperability between them. Norms or standards lay out the technical rules that must be respected by each entity in order to enable this interoperability. When a patent covers some of these rules, it is called an "essential patent" (or SEP, for Standard Essential Patent) because one cannot comply with the standard without reproducing the patented subject matter. In such a case, infringement is inevitable. Therefore, an essential patent is a formidable weapon because its owner could theoretically prevent a third party from marketing any products that comply with the standard. To mitigate this situation, standard-setting organizations generally ask holders of essential patents to declare them and to agree to license them out to any interested party under fair, reasonable and non-discriminatory conditions ("FRAND" licenses). The question, then, is what a FRAND license means in practical terms. In particular, what kind of royalty rate could be considered FRAND? When the owner of an essential patent and an implementer of the standard cannot agree on this issue, can the latter be prevented from marketing a product complying with the standard by the former on the grounds of infringement? These questions – and many others – are at the core of rich and intense litigation, which is currently developing in the world's main jurisdictions. Each group of stakeholders is trying to push the case law in a direction that is favorable to them while accusing the opposing group of not playing by the FRAND rules. Thus, holders of essential patents are often accused of trying to impose licenses on non-FRAND terms under the threat of injunctions prohibiting exploitation (*hold-up*). At the same time, implementers of standards are suspected of using various tactics to try to avoid taking licenses (*hold-out*).

While computer science and telecommunications have created new and complex problems, this could be just a preview of what is to come with what some already consider to be the fourth Industrial Revolution. This revolution is largely based on the new black gold of our time: data. Huge quantities of data (*big data*) are now being generated by billions of individuals around the world, either voluntarily (via their publications on social networks or other digital tools) or against their will (via their capture by omnipresent tracking tools). In addition to these digital traces left by people, there is also data exchanged directly between connected objects using ever more extensive networks known as the *"Internet of Things"* (IoT).

According to the European Patent Office, devices that communicate with each other through autonomous real-time data sharing will already account for a quarter of the whole Internet traffic by 2025!

The strength of the digital wave we are facing lies in the fact that we have not only data, but also powerful means to collect and store them (*cloud computing*), ensure their traceability (*blockchain*), and utilize them, for example by transforming them into material objects (*3D printing*) or by processing them so as to obtain a concrete result (*artificial intelligence*). The synergetic combination of these technologies offers almost unlimited possibilities in all fields.

As far as patents are concerned, this new landscape is a source of both new opportunities and perilous challenges. For instance, the interconnection of all objects blurs the boundaries between technical fields. An intelligent vehicle has become nothing more than a computer with connected sensors that is incidentally mounted on wheels! Litigation involving essential telecom patents has already started against car manufacturers who are not accustomed to this type of attack, and may soon extend to many other fields as well.

3D printing has the potential to change every individual into a manufacturer of products perfectly suited to their personal needs. However, this undeniable progress dilutes legal responsibilities. When the printed object is protected by a patent, can the end user be considered an infringer, even though the act performed in a private setting and for non-commercial purposes is generally lawful? If not, the patentee may be deprived of an effective means of protection, as preventing the 3D model file from circulating to users may be difficult.

Blockchain is a technology that allows the tracking of transactions in a decentralized and secure way (e.g. cryptocurrency payments that do not use a bank as an intermediary). This method seems to be of interest in the field of intellectual property, for example because it could enable patent operators to date and authenticate uses, rights or transactions without calling for large administrative support. By using blockchain in their processes, patent offices could certainly become more efficient and limit their administrative costs. However, by doing so, they would also prove that a fully centralized mode of operation is not optimal. Decentralization could expand, perhaps even to the point of calling into question the need for a central authority. To be able to survive, the offices might have no choice but to offer, for the most part, differentiating, personalized and high value-added services.

The case of artificial intelligence (AI) is perhaps the most interesting because of its ability to intrude everywhere and transform everything we previously took for granted. AI is, first of all, an integral part of a growing number of inventions, whatever their technical field. In that respect, it is itself becoming an *object* of patents, which raises the question of whether and when an invention implementing AI is patentable. The question is sensitive and similar to that of the patentability of software discussed above. One can therefore expect difficulties in this field or, alternatively, an alignment of the patentability regime of AI with that of software (of which AI would be a particular case). The European Patent Office seems to be currently moving in the direction of such an alignment.

An additional complexity lies, however, in the inherent difficulty of describing precisely how an AI produces an output from input data. Words may not be sufficient to describe this particularly complex process in detail. This raises the question of whether an AI-based invention can reasonably meet the "sufficient of disclosure" criterion (i.e. the invention must be described in such a way that a person skilled in the art can reproduce it), which is a key provision in patent systems. While lowering the bar on this criterion for AI-based inventions would be detrimental to future innovation, maintaining it would risk preventing a growing sector of innovation from accessing patent protection.

But AI is not only an object of patents. It can also become a *subject* of patents. This is at least what Stephen L. Thaler wanted to see recognized when filing patent applications in several countries with an AI named DABUS (*Device for the Autonomous Bootstrapping of Unified Sentience*) listed as sole inventor. According to Thaler, the claimed inventions – which relate respectively to a food container and a flashing light for attracting enhanced attention – were indeed generated autonomously by an AI based on neural networks. The patent offices therefore have to decide whether an AI can be a full-fledged inventor. At this stage, the European, U.S. and British patent offices (as well as the British courts) have answered in the negative, determining that an inventor must be a natural person, i.e. a human. In South Africa and Australia, on the other hand, AI systems have initially been recognized as legitimate inventors. The question certainly divisive.

Accepting that an AI can be an inventor would remove the last remnants of moral justification for the patent since there is no inventive effort on the part of a machine that the patent would reward. The patent would then fall definitively into the utilitarian domain, meaning it would become a tool deployed only in service of the economy. In the absence of any moral element, however, one may wonder whether it would still be socially acceptable to regard patent infringement as a reprehensible act.

Accepting the idea that an AI could invent autonomously poses another major problem. As we have seen previously, according to the current laws, an invention must be inventive to be patentable. In other words, it must not be obvious to a person skilled in the art. This criterion refers to the intellectual capacities of an average person. On the other hand, in a world where AIs, which potentially have access to the entire state of the art in the world, are capable of inventing, how can we distinguish what is obvious from what is not? The performance of AIs is constantly improving and it is conceivable that the AIs of the future will surpass human capabilities, including in the field of invention. If this is indeed the case, it could be argued, as Professor Ryan Abbott does, that "everything is obvious" from an AI's point of view. If no invention can pass the bar of inventive step anymore, it may simply mean the end of patents.

Despite the serious threats that AI poses to patents, one should not overlook the benefits that it can also provide them. In addition to its object and subject functions mentioned above, AI may also become a unique *means* to improve patent procedures on multiple levels. AIs have already been used to assist in patent drafting. Others have been proposed to perform statistical analysis on decisions issued by patent offices or courts, or to help identify case law relevant and comparable to a given legal situation. These tools can be used, for example, for "predictive justice" purposes to better prepare a litigation case.

But where AI could prove most useful is in assisting prior art searches. These searches are tedious because they require the finding of correlations between technical descriptions that are sometimes long, complex and based on different terms and angles of approach. AI seems particularly well suited to identifying correlations within a large corpus of documentation and selecting only the few closest references to which a human can subsequently attend. By improving the efficiency of prior art searches, AI could greatly facilitate the work of patent offices. It could also clean up the patent landscape by avoiding the granting (or by enabling the invalidation) of patents covering inventions which are not new or not inventive.

Only time will tell whether the technologies of the fourth Industrial Revolution will improve or defeat patents.

UNITED STATES PATENT OFFICE.

FELIX HOFFMANN, OF ELBERFELD, GERMANY, ASSIGNOR TO THE FARBEN-
FABRIKEN OF ELBERFELD COMPANY, OF NEW YORK.

ACETYL SALICYLIC ACID.

SPECIFICATION forming part of Letters Patent No. 644,077, dated February 27, 1900.

Application filed August 1, 1898. Serial No. 687,385. (Specimens.)

To all whom it may concern:

Be it known that I, FELIX HOFFMANN, doctor of philosophy, chemist, (assignor to the FARBENFABRIKEN OF ELBERFELD COMPANY,
5 of New York,) residing at Elberfeld, Germany, have invented a new and useful Improvement in the Manufacture or Production of Acetyl Salicylic Acid; and I hereby declare the following to be a clear and exact description of
10 my invention.

In the *Annalen der Chemie und Pharmacie*, Vol. 150, pages 11 and 12, Kraut has described that he obtained by the action of acetyl chlorid on salicylic acid a body which he thought to
15 be acetyl salicylic acid. I have now found that on heating salicylic acid with acetic anhydride a body is obtained the properties of which are perfectly different from those of the body described by Kraut. According to my
20 researches the body obtained by means of my new process is undoubtedly the real acetyl salicylic acid

$$C_6H_4\begin{cases}OCO.CH_3\\COOH.\end{cases}$$

Therefore the compound described by Kraut cannot be the real acetyl salicylic acid, but
30 is another compound. In the following I point out specifically the principal differences between my new compound and the body described by Kraut.

If the Kraut product is boiled even for a
35 long while with water, (according to Kraut's statement,) acetic acid is not produced, while my new body when boiled with water is readily split up, acetic and salicylic acid being produced. The watery solution of the Kraut
40 body shows the same behavior on the addition of a small quantity of ferric chlorid as a watery solution of salicylic acid when mixed with a small quantity of ferric chlorid—that is to say, it assumes a violet color. On the
45 contrary, a watery solution of my new body when mixed with ferric chlorid does not assume a violet color. If a melted test portion of the Kraut body is allowed to cool, it begins to solidify (according to Kraut's statement)
50 at from 118° to 118.5° centigrade, while a melted test portion of my product solidifies at about 70° centigrade. The melting-points of the two compounds cannot be compared, be-

cause Kraut does not give the melting-point of his compound. It follows from these de-
55 tails that the two compounds are absolutely different.

In producing my new compound I can proceed as follows, (without limiting myself to the particulars given:) A mixture prepared
60 from fifty parts of salicylic acid and seventy-five parts of acetic anhydride is heated for about two hours at about 150° centigrade in a vessel provided with a reflux condenser. Thus a clear liquid is obtained, from which
65 on cooling a crystalline mass is separated, which is the acetyl salicylic acid. It is freed from the acetic anhydride by pressing and then recrystallized from dry chloroform. The acid is thus obtained in the shape of glitter-
70 ing white needles melting at about 135° centigrade, which are easily soluble in benzene, alcohol, glacial acetic acid, and chloroform, but difficultly soluble in cold water. It has the formula

$$C_6H_4\begin{cases}OCOCH_3\\COOH\end{cases}$$

and exhibits therapeutical properties.

Having now described my invention and in
80 what manner the same is to be performed, what I claim as new, and desire to secure by Letters Patent, is—

As a new article of manufacture the acetyl salicylic acid having the formula:

$$C_6H_4\begin{cases}O.COCH_3\\COOH\end{cases}$$

being when crystallized from dry chloroform
90 in the shape of white glittering needles, easily soluble in benzene, alcohol and glacial acetic acid, difficultly soluble in cold water, being split by hot water into acetic acid and salicylic acid, melting at about 135° centigrade, sub-
95 stantially as hereinbefore described.

In testimony whereof I have signed my name in the presence of two subscribing witnesses.

FELIX HOFFMANN.

Witnesses:
R. E. JAHN,
OTTO KÖNIG.

U.S. patent on Aspirin granted in 1900 to Felix Hoffmann,
a chemist employed by the company Bayer

Source: Espacenet - Public domain

248

HEALTH CHALLENGES

THE PATENT IN THE FACE OF THE PANDEMIC

If there is one perfect area where patents raise questions, it is in the field of health. An essential mission for every state is to guarantee the health of its citizens and, therefore, to facilitate the optimal production and distribution of medicines (and other inventions that serve a therapeutic or prophylactic purpose). In theory, anything that might impede the achievement of this goal should be removed. The moral imperative of saving lives and ensuring human welfare should prevail over any economic considerations. However, by giving private laboratories control over certain treatments, patents are sometimes perceived as the obstacle to be removed. Does this mean that medicines are incompatible with the patent mechanism?

In fact, medicines have not always been protectable by patents. For example, although the first French patent law of 1791 did not include an exemption, its 1844 revision excluded "pharmaceutical compositions and remedies of all kinds" from patentability. Similar exclusions existed elsewhere in Europe at the same time, but not in the United States. In the early 19th century, the manufacture of medicines was carried out exclusively in pharmacies by the pharmacists themselves, who were opposed to the granting of patents because it would have caused them to lose control over this activity. Pharmacists proposed that medicines should benefit humanity and not be used for profit. Their arguments were considered more convincing than those of other scientists, such as the chemist and physicist Gay-Lussac, who stressed the importance of protecting the rights of inventors and creating a real pharmaceutical industry.

It was not until a century later at the end of the Second World War that things changed again. By then, pharmaceutical companies had formed that were capable of producing standardized drugs on a large scale. They adopted new ways of organizing work and strengthened their research and development activities to match the practices of other industries such as chemistry and electricity. For the pharmaceutical industry, this convergence justified benefitting from the same rights available to other fields, particularly regarding the protection of innovations.

After a transitional phase, medicines finally became patentable again in the same way as other French products in 1968. The same phenomenon can also be observed in many other countries, notably as a result of the TRIPS Agreement of 1994, which required that patents be granted in all technological fields including pharmaceuticals.

Nevertheless, the health sector remains unique. Medicines are not a commodity like any other. Their users are patients, not mere consumers. The state is more present in this sector than in many others, for instance through mechanisms of social protection and health insurance. In the case of patents, the law is adapted to take into account the specificities of this industry. Certain legal provisions limit the scope of patent law in the health sector. For example, some states can impose "compulsory licenses" (mentioned above) for public health reasons, allowing a third party to produce or use the subject matter of a patent without the authorization of the holder. On the contrary, other adjustments to patent law aim to compensate for factors that disadvantage drug developers. In European Union states, the special title awarded by the "supplementary protection certificate" extends by several years the duration of protection for a product used in the composition of a medicine or a phytopharmaceutical product covered by a patent. This compensates for the time required to obtain marketing authorization for new drugs, which can significantly encroach on the maximum 20-year patent term. The law therefore seems to have struck a balance adapted to the specifics of the sector by providing mechanisms for the protection of public health while also giving pharmaceutical companies the means to make their investments profitable. This balance is perhaps one of the reasons why patents are particularly efficient in the pharmaceutical field, as we have seen in a previous chapter.

Given that life sciences have progressively intruded into the health field, it is worth mentioning here that their patentability was recognized fairly recently. This shift is usually traced back to the 1980 U.S. Supreme Court decision in the case of *Diamond v. Chakrabarty*, which is famous for having expressed the idea that "anything under the sun that is made by man" should be protectable by patent. This decision is considered to have contributed to the development of biotechnology. Once the United States had opened this breach, other countries, especially in Europe, had no choice but to follow suit to avoid being left behind.

Throughout the writing of this book, the first pandemic of the 21st century, Covid-19, is still raging after nearly two years. First appearing in China in late 2019, the virus quickly spread across the globe, plunging the world into a health crisis resembling one of the worst science fiction scenarios imaginable. Overnight, millions of people were confined, many hospitals were saturated, and entire sectors of the economy were devastated. Scientists around the world have worked hard to prevent a disaster, and the pharmaceutical industry has moved into high gear to find effective cures. Helped by a rapid sequencing of the virus genome, laboratories have developed the first vaccines. A race against time for vaccination was initiated to limit the number of victims as the virus continued to spread.

In this anxious context, accusing eyes quickly turned to the patent. Patents were suspected of slowing down the deployment of vaccines – considered to be a global common good – and preventing their equitable distribution in all countries regardless of their level of wealth. Voices have been raised demanding that patents related to this new disease be "waived". In October 2020, India and South Africa officially asked the WTO to suspend certain binding provisions of the TRIPS Agreement on a temporary basis. This move has been gaining support from more and more countries, culminating in the unprecedented support of U.S. President Joe Biden in May 2021.

While we are still in the midst of the crisis, it is impossible to draw definitive conclusions with regard to the role of patents in the situation due to a lack of hindsight and reliable data. Moreover, the seriousness of the subject requires caution. I will therefore simply provide some food for thought, leaving it to the researchers to carry out an in-depth analysis in due course.

The first point to note is that, for the first time in history, vaccines were developed very quickly after the onset of the disease with only a 10 months for the first to be generated. By comparison, it took 5 years to develop a vaccine against Ebola. Furthermore, not only one Covid-19 vaccine has been administered, but more than a dozen are already in circulation. According to data from the World Health Organization (WHO), as of November 2021, no less than 135 vaccine candidates are in clinical development and 194 are in preclinical development! Some of these vaccines are based on traditional technologies that inoculate against a modified virus, while others rely on the more recent messenger RNA (mRNA) technology that uses a molecule of genetic information that causes the production of a viral protein that activates the immune system. The mRNA vaccines have proven to be particularly effective (over 90%, compared to 60% for conventional flu vaccines) and they appear to have had relatively few side effects to date.

This small miracle is due primarily to science and research excellence of course, but also to the health ecosystem that created the conditions for it to happen. Among the elements that have contributed to this success are the huge amounts of capital, both public and private, invested in research, as well as the financial support of organizations such as the *Biomedical Advanced Research and Development Authority* (BARDA), an office of the U.S. Department of Health and Human Services created in 2006 specifically to fight bioterrorism and pandemics. Has the patent also been one of the factors that enabled the active development of effective and innovative vaccines? This cannot be ruled out. At the very least, it has not prevented this outcome.

Likewise, it has not prevented the eventuation of several hundred partnerships between drug companies. Given the role of the patent in accelerating cooperation, as we have seen previously, it has likely even fostered these partnerships. One example is the successful partnership formed in September 2020 between the German company BioNTech and the pharmaceutical giant Pfizer. Some of the cooperations that have emerged may seem unnatural, for example when Sanofi made its production capacity and teams available to bottle the vaccine produced by its competitor Pfizer. The same is true of the South African company Aspen, which bottles doses for the American laboratory Johnson & Johnson and may soon be manufacturing and selling the vaccine under its own brand. Would such voluntary cooperations have been possible without the protection offered by the patent? Nothing is less certain.

But the patent is not only an accelerator for cooperation; it is also a tool for exclusion. This may raise concerns that a patent holder could attempt to block the manufacture or distribution of Covid-19 vaccines. While this scenario is theoretically possible, it seems unlikely that a patentee would risk degrading its image by suggesting it would be ready to put human lives at risk to enforce its rights. In March 2020, the licensing company Labrador Diagnostic LLC sued the diagnostic company bioMérieux which produces tests for Covid-19, for patent infringement. Although Labrador made it publicly clear that its action targeted infectious diseases unrelated to Covid-19, it faced an outpouring of hate in the press and on social media, which compared it to pure evil. To appease the public, the company then committed to not collect royalties from anyone developing tests for Covid-19. As long as the pandemic continues, it is even harder to imagine that any major pharmaceutical company would request an injunction against a vaccine for patent infringement. In this regard, it is interesting to note that, as early as October 2020, Moderna has publicly promised not to use its patents against companies producing Covid-19 vaccines. Should a patent infringement action nevertheless be filed, we can only hope that the courts would issue a decision that preserves public health.

In addition to the injunction risk, another critique of the patent has been launched, claiming it would both slow down the production of vaccines by reserving such capacities to a limited number of players and prevent their equitable distribution throughout the world in order to maximize profits. These accusations are probably based on the general ability of patent holders to control their markets, but there is no objective data to back up such an assessment in the present case. However, it can be noted that many production capacities are already being mobilized in addition to those of the major vaccine suppliers, as illustrated by the example of Sanofi mentioned above.

More than 6 billion doses of vaccine were produced from January to August 2021. At the current pace, 12 billion doses must have been reached by the end of 2021 and, if all goes well, a doubling could occur in the following 6 months. Despite a (probably inevitable) slow start, the quantities produced seem to be on track to cover global needs.

Regarding vaccine distribution, there are indeed significant inequalities in access between countries with different levels of wealth. As of December 2021, 68% of vaccine doses had been distributed in only ten countries, according to the WHO, while only 30% of vaccines had been distributed in the low- and middle-income countries that represent 51% of the world's population. Although donations and transfers of doses to developing countries have occurred (both directly from developed countries and through the Covax initiative designed to accelerate the development, production and equitable access to Covid-19 tests, treatments and vaccines), they appear to be largely insufficient. This poses a serious problem for populations lacking doses in the first place and also increases the risk of virus mutations. Are patents responsible for this state of affairs? This could only be the case if relevant patents had been granted in most developing countries, which seems unlikely. Indeed, the Covid-19 genome was sequenced in January 2020. Assuming that patents were filed right after this sequencing, they are unlikely to have been issued yet because of the usual length of the procedure. It is possible, however, that older relevant but non-Covid-19-specific patents are in the hands of the major vaccine suppliers, but such patents are likely to affect only a limited number of developing countries.

Furthermore, one cannot overlook other causes that have impacted access to vaccines in a more obvious way than patents. In particular, there have been many logistical challenges, especially in producing, transporting and storing mRNA vaccines at very low temperatures. The lack of trained staff to deliver the vaccines under satisfactory conditions also appears to have had a negative impact. Some countries declared a "national preference" and banned the export of vaccines or some of their components as long as they considered their vaccination coverage insufficient. Finally, mistrust towards the new vaccines has created a glass ceiling for vaccination rates in many societies.

Assuming that patents have somehow impeded the equitable deployment of vaccines, could "waiving" them improve the situation? This is indeed a hypothesis based on the idea that companies could start producing and distributing, without the risk of infringing, generic vaccines that would come in addition to the doses produced by patent-holding laboratories. If these generic manufacturers were located as close as possible to disadvantaged populations, immunization could be improved. However, this presupposes that these generic manufacturers are capable of rapidly producing effective vaccines that meet all quality standards. For mRNA vaccines, however, the skills required can be difficult and time-consuming to develop, which offsets the advantage of diversifying production sources.

On the other hand, waiving patents poses a major problem in the middle term, because of its very broad scope. Indeed, the proposal submitted to the WTO amounts in reality to abolishing, for at least 3 years, all intellectual property rights relating to everything that concerns the fight against Covid-19. Such a waiver of existing rights is already problematic as far as patents are concerned, since it would suddenly break the balance of power discussed above by disadvantaging the current operators over the innovators of the future. The laboratories that have successfully developed the vaccines that are saving lives, at the cost of taking very significant risks and making considerable investment (which probably includes paying royalties for prior mRNA patents), would thus be deprived of the competitive advantage they were counting on in the long term.

However, the most serious problem relates not to patents, but to secret know-how, which is also targeted by the "waiving" of rights requested from the WTO. Indeed, as we have seen, once a secret is revealed, its original holder instantly loses control of it and of its associated value. Even if the waiver of rights is temporary, the secret can never be effectively restored. Given the complexity of the new mRNA technology, waiving rights on the secret know-how would therefore amount to asking Pfizer, BioNTech, Moderna and others to expend resources on training any interested third party in the knowledge accumulated over years of research. The trained third parties could then become serious competitors in the future. Likewise, even if confidentiality or non-competition commitments were required, there would be no guarantee that they are kept, especially if the third parties in question are located in countries that generally do not respect intellectual property rights. It is therefore understandable that some developed countries are reluctant to penalize their national pharmaceutical industry so severely and permanently, even in the name of the fight against the pandemic. Moreover, as we have seen earlier, inventions naturally tend to concentrate on fields where effective protection is possible. If neither patents nor secrecy were respected in the field of Covid-19, we could well see big pharma players move away from this sector, considering it too risky and therefore unattractive. This would be very bad news at a time when the pandemic is still active and when excellent research is more necessary than ever to develop effective drugs in addition to the vaccines already available, and to fight against the future variants and/or other diseases that will surely continue to appear in the future.

Are there mechanisms other than a "waiver" of intellectual property rights that could improve the health situation without harming the pharmaceutical industry? The TRIPS Agreement does indeed contain provisions allowing each country to grant compulsory licenses on public health grounds. These provisions have been used several times in the past, notably in the fight against the HIV virus. At the beginning of the Covid-19 pandemic, some countries, such as Canada, Israel, Germany, Ecuador and Chile, also used them. Compulsory licenses have several advantages over waiving intellectual property rights. Firstly, they are limited to patent rights and do not affect secret know-how. They also include several limitations and conditions, such as the need to provide reasonable compensation to patent holders. As an exceptional system, they can only be used as a last resort (e.g. after direct negotiations between the parties have failed). Provided for in the TRIPS Agreement itself, they are an application – rather than a circumvention – of the law. However, neither do compulsory licenses come without flaws. In particular, their implementation can take time and be laborious, and because they apply nationally they cannot be made globally uniform. Though imperfect, compulsory licenses nevertheless represent a more realistic option than a patent "waiver".

The key to the fight against the pandemic certainly lies in the ability to show solidarity and responsibility at all levels. The pharmaceutical industry is no exception to this principle and must behave in an exemplary manner. In times of crisis, patents cannot be used exactly as they would be in normal times. Their plasticity can be an advantage in this respect, and their role in accelerating cooperations must be fully exploited to make vaccines and future medicines accessible to all without delay. At the same time, their exclusionary function must be limited, either on the initiative of their holders themselves or, failing that, by restrictive measures. It is important, however, to avoid going too far in challenging a system that could still prove useful during other possible health issues to come.

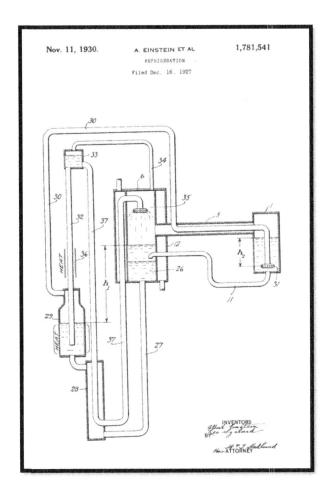

Patent granted to Electrolux Servel Corporation in 1931
for an apparatus and a refrigeration process
invented by Albert Einstein and Leo Szilard

Szilard was one of the physicists who convinced Einstein to warn the United
States that the Nazi Germany might use nuclear fission to make bombs.

GEOPOLITICAL CHALLENGES

THE PATENT: A STAKE IN INTERNATIONAL RELATIONS

We have seen previously that at the national level, each state shapes its patent system according to its economic interests. However, the national interest of one state is rarely compatible with that of others, which can be a source of conflict. When states perceive that they have more to gain by cooperating than by competing, they generally do so. As a result, patents sometimes give rise to cooperation and sometimes to rivalry between states.

First of all, in recent years, the major patent offices have tended to work more collaboratively. An initiative known as "IP5" brings together the offices of Europe, the United States, Japan, South Korea and China – which together account for 80% of all patent applications worldwide – around a common program for greater harmonization of practices and procedures, enhanced work-sharing, high-quality and timely search and examination results, and seamless access to patent information.

In addition, bilateral agreements are regularly signed between patent offices to improve the efficiency of procedures and avoid redundancies. For example, *"Patent Prosecution Highway"* (PPH) programs ensure that the results of the examination of a patent application by a first office are used in the subsequent examination by a second office, with the aim of speeding up the procedure and improving the reliability of the delivered results. While each national office continues to conduct its own examinations, the streamlining enabled by the PPH programs represents a further step towards joint examination by several independent states and, maybe one day, a single worldwide examination process. It is interesting to note that these developments are spontaneous and not part of international agreements. States have an interest in setting up these cooperative ventures, which save them resources without eroding their sovereignty.

This increase in the number of patent cooperations does, however, not prevent rivalries from arising between states. While these rivalries are most often of low intensity, they occasionally take on harsher forms as parts of larger conflicts.

In particular, a rivalry has emerged and grown between developed and developing countries. As we have seen in previous chapters, there were a great diversity of patent systems throughout the world at the end of the 19th century, with each country having shaped its system according to its own needs. The harmonization that followed, as a result of international treaties being signed, blurred the differences between systems. However, this harmonization took place at the initiative of the most industrialized countries and generally worked in the direction of strengthening the rights of patentees (via extension of the scope of patentability, geographical expansion, limitation of protectionist measures, etc.). In less developed countries, this strengthening may have benefited primarily foreign manufacturers and slowed down the emergence of innovative national industries. The realization of this phenomenon towards the end of the 20th century led to frustration, because developing countries had accepted the rules of harmonization in the hope (and promise) that they would benefit domestic industry. In response, developed countries were accused of "neo-colonialism". This accusation is exacerbated by the fact that it is almost impossible now to return to the prior situation because, in today's globalized economy, if a country were to abolish patents it would risk being marginalized. Resolving this confrontation between the Global North and South would require allowing for more flexibility in the application of international treaties such that each state could freely adapt its patent system to meet its own needs without demolishing the entire edifice.

Rivalries also exist between developed countries, many of which strive either directly or indirectly to increase their "patent activity" from year to year. Indeed, to have a strong patent position makes it possible to offer the image of a country focused on innovation and growth, which is likely to attract worldwide investors to the detriment of countries that look less innovative. Thus, a tacit competition takes place between developed countries to surpass the others in the number of national patent applications submitted.

For several years now, we have also seen a more direct involvement of governments looking to push national industry and make it competitive. For example, sovereign funds have been created by some states in order to proactively help domestic companies to build their patent portfolio. Some of these funds have even generated a surprising activity where the patent portfolios of several domestic companies are grouped into coherent technological clusters that are then licensed out to foreign companies so as to generate revenue for the benefit of national industry. This is the case, for example, with the investment fund France Brevets, created in 2011 by the

French state, the National Research Agency and the Caisse des dépôts et consignations. Within this set-up, the French State serves as an active and biased intermediary between domestic patent owners and potential foreign users.

Competition between developed countries also exists in the field of litigation. Since companies often have a choice in the judicial forum to which they take their patent cases, some countries may be tempted to attract litigation suits by various means. When the same case is tried in parallel in several jurisdictions around the world, the judges in different countries study the decisions of their foreign counterpart in order to either draw inspiration from them or to distinguish themselves from them as appropriate. They compete among themselves to issue the judgment that is, for instance, the most thorough, the most severe on infringers, or the most creative.

Litigation in the field of essential telecom patents offers a particularly instructive example of this rivalry between the jurisdictions of different countries. Indeed, as patents are national in scope, the court of a country typically rules on the validity and/or infringement of a patent within the bounds of its national territory. However, since the usual practice in essential patent matters is to negotiate licenses on a global basis rather than by country, courts in some states have taken the position that it is within their jurisdiction to define and impose the terms of a global FRAND license. This is the case in the United Kingdom (see e.g. *Unwired Planet v. Huawei* and *Conversant v. Huawei & ZTE*) and in China (see e.g. *Sharp Corporation v. OPPO et al.*). This development, which challenges the traditional geographical jurisdiction of the courts, may completely change the nature of global litigation. Indeed, holders of essential patents who wish to avoid multiple parallel litigations may prefer to bring their cases to courts with self-appointed global jurisdiction. However, courts in other countries might then follow the same path so as not to be deprived of national litigation opportunities. If this happens, courts could all compete with each other on a global scale. The courts of each state could thus attempt to take over one another's cases by being particularly favorable to the plaintiffs or by other means.

The battle between jurisdictions has recently taken on an even more direct form through legal actions known as "*Anti-suit injunctions*" (ASIs). These ASI actions aim to obtain from a court in country A that it forbids an opposing party from initiating or continuing a lawsuit before a court in country B. For example, courts, especially in China, have supported such ASI actions to prevent patent disputes from being brought into foreign jurisdictions. However, sovereign courts do not appreciate foreign attempts to prevent them from dispensing justice as they see fit. Thus, in response to ASIs, so-called "*Anti-anti suit injunctions*" (AASIs) have arisen whereby the court of country B intends to counter the effect of the prior ASI issued in country A. In a case opposing IPCom and Lenovo in 2020, the Paris Court of Appeal issued such an AASI preventing the enforcement of an ASI previously requested in the United States. Taking the logic and its escalation even further, attempts of AAASI and even AAAASI actions have begun to emerge. The global fight for the respect of judicial jurisdiction and national sovereignty has probably never been so lively, which proves the high stakes of patent litigation for the states involved in this battle.

Sometimes, rivalries between states can turn into real confrontations. The patent may then be only one aspect of a broader conflict. This is what is currently happening between the United States and China, whose dissents find one of their justifications in intellectual property. Although the U.S. was the absolute master of innovation in the world for a long time, a sense of slowing down is now spreading in the country as China gains strength. As shown in particular by its "*Made in China 2025*" plan, China is no longer hiding its ambitions for technological domination in strategic areas such as 5G telephony, artificial intelligence, semiconductors, aerospace and biotechnology.

China's fast-paced technological development is certainly apparent in the field of intellectual property. As early as 2011, the Chinese patent office overtook the U.S. to become the office receiving the most patent applications in the world. Over the past decade, this gap has widened significantly. According to data published by WIPO, China's weight in the number of patent filings worldwide rose from 19.6% in 2010 to 45.7% in 2020, a year in which the Chinese office received no less than 1.5 million applications, which is 2.5 times the number of filings made in the same year in the U.S. Admittedly, part of the reason for this deviation is the difference in demographics between the two countries; however, even as a ratio to GDP, China's numbers now exceed those of the U.S. Nonetheless, in 2020 the two countries were still neck and neck in terms of total national patents in force, with 3.3 million in the U.S. and 3.1 million in China, the latter enjoying stronger annual growth.

The breakthrough of China is also visible in the international PCT system, to which the country has become the largest contributor in terms of annual filings (more than 69,500 from China, compared to just over 59,500 from the U.S. in 2021). Unsurprisingly, the largest PCT filer in 2021 was a Chinese company with 6,952 PCT applications or 2.5% of the total. This company was telecom equipment maker Huawei, the same company that the Trump administration blacklisted in 2019 after accusing it of undermining U.S. national security. There is political continuity in America in this regard, as the Biden administration revoked the license of operator China Telecom America on similar grounds in October 2021.

Given the staggering numbers mentioned above, it is understandable that some Americans are nervous about the rising power of China. This feeling is reinforced by the perception, on the American side, that China has reached this level of sophistication through unfair means, notably by violating and stealing American intellectual property, as President Trump regularly claimed. In addition, massive patent (as well as trademark) filings in China saturate the system, to the detriment of "real" innovators. American specialists consider that the number of Chinese filings is artificially inflated by exogenous, non-market factors such as disproportionate public subsidies, the setting of high targets for public institutions or the existence of filings made in bad faith. According to this theory, intellectual property rights in China are greater in quantity but much lower in quality and commercial value than those of the United States. Evidence of this would be found in the low rate of Chinese inventions resulting in commercialized innovations, as well as in the low proportion of Chinese inventions that are patented in other countries. For example, in 2020, China filed only about 100,000 patent applications abroad, that is, no more than Germany. This is less than 7% of what it files domestically. Similarly, China was responsible for only 7% of European patent filings in 2020, compared to 25% for the U.S.

For its part, China vigorously defends itself against such American accusations and puts forwards its desire to achieve technological independence through national innovation. In response to criticism that cites the low quality of its intellectual property titles, China regularly changes its law. A fourth amendment to China's patent law was passed in June 2021 to introduce several improvements that move toward strengthening patents. In another sign that China is not insensitive to critique, in early 2021 the country announced that it would end all government subsidies of patents by 2025.

Of course, the tensions between China and the United States have multiple causes and are manifested in various sectors, including the military field. It is however interesting to note that they are now expressed more specifically and explicitly around intellectual property. The fact that intellectual property and patents figure prominently in the rhetoric of the conflict between two powers vying for technological supremacy says something about the strategic importance that these tools have acquired in international relations in the 21st century. As Chinese Premier Wen Jiabao announced back in 2006: "the competition of the future world is a competition for intellectual property rights".

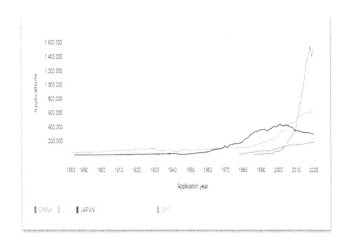

Number of patent applications filed with the five main offices
(China, U.S., Japan, South Korea, Europe) between 1883 and 2020

The upward trend since the 1980s is remarkable.

Source: WIPO, *World Intellectual Property Indicators 2021* -
https://www.wipo.int/edocs/pubdocs/en/wipo_pub_941_2021.pdf

INFLATIONARY CHALLENGE

THE PATENT TO THE TEST OF LARGE NUMBERS

3.2 million. That is the number of new patent applications filed worldwide in 2019, according to WIPO data. This represents a near doubling in just fifteen years. If we add the 2.3 million utility models (titles that are generally easier to obtain and of shorter term than patents), we reach 5.5 million applications for protection of technical inventions in 2019, which corresponds to a tripling in fifteen years. In total, there were no less than 15 million patents and 5.6 million utility models in force worldwide in 2019.

As the diagram at the beginning of this chapter illustrates, the number of patent applications filed annually remained relatively stable for almost a century following 1883. Initially moderate growth then began to appear before accelerating in the 1980s. The example of the United States speaks for itself: in May 2021, the country issued its 11,000,000th patent, 231 years after the creation of the U.S. patent system in 1790. However, it was not until 1910 (after 120 years) that the 1,000,000th patent was granted. Since then, each additional million patents has been issued after a shorter and shorter period of time. Less than 3 years passed between the 10 millionth granted in 2018 and the 11 millionth that has just been reached. This acceleration is startling.

And this is nothing compared to China. From 173,000 patent applications in 2005, the number grew to 1.5 million for the year 2020, an increase to the factor of 9 in just 15 years. As the above diagram shows, China's exponential curve has crushed all others, almost erasing the fact that the European Patent Office has seen its number of filings grow by 40% over the same period. Only Japan seems to be experiencing a continuous decrease in patent filings since the early 2000s (after a remarkable growth over the previous 30 years and with still nearly 200,000 applications filed in 2019). The current weight of Asia is particularly impressive, with the continent having received two thirds of the new applications filed globally in 2020 (compared to 19.3% for North America and 10.9% for Europe).

What do these large numbers tell us? First, that patent activity is doing well both in Asia and elsewhere in the world. As patents protect new and inventive inventions, the growth in filings seems to indicate that innovation is booming. This is generally good news for humanity, which, thanks to this abundance of innovation, can access products and services that improve life in all fields: health, transportation, communications, leisure, etc. Even when considering that a portion of the patents filed would be the result of company strategies that do not directly benefit society, the influence of technical progress on the growth of patent figures cannot be overlooked.

However, such an acceleration in the pace of filings does not come without consequence for the balance of the patent system. It is easy to picture how the system works when a single patent (or a small number of patents) covers a market: players wishing to be present on the market can either try to get a license from the patent holder or try to design around the patented solution by alternative technical means. In both cases, they can operate without undue hindrance. But what happens when not a few patents, but myriad patents cover the market in question?

The answer to this question has been theorized by economists as the "tragedy of the anti-commons". In contrast to common goods, whose uncontrolled use can give rise to abuses and excesses, the anti-commons – which are goods covered by a multitude of independent private property titles – can become unusable when their legal use would require the authorization of many owners, each of which holds blocking power. This is the case with patents: when a product or process is covered by a large number of patents (some of which may relate to fairly marginal aspects), it becomes unrealistic for a new entrant to the market to obtain authorization from every patent holder. In addition to the enormous identification and negotiation work that would be involved, such an approach would not even necessarily be economically viable, since each patent holder can demand licensing fees without taking into consideration the financial asks of the others. The result is a situation of royalty stacking that could prevent the prospective operation from being profitable.

These risks are not just theoretical; the telecom sector offers a real example. The number of active patents covering a smartphone is estimated to be in the tens or even hundreds of thousands. On the pure telephony side alone, since 2015, 150,000 patents have been declared essential for the implementation of the 5G standard. And that does not include patents covering user interface aspects, Bluetooth, WiFi, GPS and the many other features built into smartphones that are deemed essential by consumers. In addition, other relevant patents apply to the network infrastructure that is necessary for smartphones to function. Furthermore, there are patents that protect related aspects, such as the processes involved in production and distribution chains. The user of a smartphone is not even aware of the staggering number of inventions behind his device, even if they appreciate the finished product.

For a new entrant, the task of launching a smartphone is almost impossible. Indeed, not only would they have to face an already established competition, but they would also have to avoid infringing upon all the existing patents. The risk of infringement is normally assessed and reduced before the launch of a product by identifying and analyzing the relevant patents in force. This "freedom to practice" work is long and complex because it requires a thorough analysis of the claims laid out by the identified patents. When faced with thousands of potentially blocking patents written in various languages, such analysis becomes impractical and the chance of finding design-arounds is slim. While new software products offer visualization tools that can help assess the patent landscape in given a field, at present they are no substitute for an in-depth study by a human analyst. As a result, the new entrant is faced with an unsatisfactory choice: either they give up their product launch project (as predicted by the tragedy of the anti-commons theory), or they decide to go ahead anyway, assuming the risk of infringement, even if it means that they will later have to withdraw their product from the market and pay damages to the infringed patent holders.

This situation, worsened by the inflation of the number of patents, is not sustainable and poses a serious problem for free competition. The barriers to entry erected through patents by the incumbent players leave no room for new entrants in certain markets. In view of the above-mentioned current patent filing numbers in China, it is clear that this problem is particularly acute for any company wishing to enter the Chinese market.

For the incumbent players themselves, the situation is also problematic. The proliferation of patents means that none of them can exploit the technology with confidence, since each one is obliged to use the patents of others.

Cross-licensing between the different players can help to break this deadlock, provided that the players can agree on the relative importance of their patent portfolios and the resulting royalties. In the absence of an agreement, a balance of terror reigns: one avoids suing their competitor for infringement for fear of being attacked in return. Breaking this balance can lead to a painful patent war for all parties involved. This has been the case since the early 2000s in the cell phone industry, where most cell phone and SIM card manufacturers have been involved in patent litigation against each other.

To solve the above-mentioned problems, companies have decided to pool their patents and offer them in bundled licenses. Such *patent pools* have emerged for various technologies such as 3GPP cell phone standards or MPEG-2 audio and video compression, among others. The introduction of patent pools specifically for standard essential patents (SEPs) has been allowed and even encouraged in several countries, despite the risk of distorting competition as a result. This is the case in Europe, as highlighted by a communication from the European Commission dated 29 November 2017. By facilitating the identification of essential patents on a given technology and allowing the negotiation of global licenses via a one-stop shop, patent pools are sometimes considered the only way to resolve blocking situations and enable new technology to reach the market. Moreover, they are supposed to reduce the total amount of license fees to be paid by users and prevent royalty stacking.

As economist Petra Moser has shown, the results of patent pools are actually ambiguous. The first pool in history seems to have been created in 1856 in the field of sewing machines to put an end to the patent war that had broken out between Elias Howe – the first patent troll, mentioned in a previous chapter –, the Singer company and two other manufacturers. According to Petra Moser, the creation of this pool has indeed limited the litigation activity between its members and reduced the total amount of royalties charged. At the same time, however, patenting activity declined and only resumed after the pool was dissolved in 1877, suggesting that the pool hindered innovation for the duration of its existence. Beyond this example, the evidence seems to confirm that a patent pool has the effect of reducing the level of competition among its members, to the detriment of the often younger and less established companies that reside outside the pool. Some pools have even resulted in lower royalties for their members than for outside companies. Faced with such a disadvantage, outside companies cannot reasonably compete with pool members and are driven away from patented technologies in favor of inferior alternative techniques. Thus, contrary to the objective pursued, the pools are likely to orient technical change in a direction unfavorable to innovation.

Even though patent pools provide some benefits, their coverage of a technology is rarely comprehensive. Patent holders will always want to stay out of the pools, as they feel they can get more out of their patent portfolios by licensing them independently. Some technologies may also be subject to several competing pools, from which users would have to take multiple respective licenses, leading to the possibly prohibitive accumulation of royalties. If there were more competing patent pools in the future, pools of patent pools (or "meta-pools") could emerge, further concentrating the power of holding patents among a select few. In the absence of strong safeguards, such concentration could lead to excessive market power that would leave no room for outsiders. On the other hand, the more members there are in a pool, the smaller the share of royalties allocated to each member, which raises the question of the economic viability of the system in the long run.

The multiplication of patents is therefore a major problem for which no ideal solution has been found to date.

This problem puts the overall balance of the patent system to the test by impacting all of its stakeholders at once. Indeed, patent holders, who are more and more in competition with each other, find it increasingly difficult to make a profit on their investments because the licensing revenues must be shared among them. Future innovators, faced with a maze of private rights, find it harder to locate free space for development and risk moving away from innovation in favor of inferior technical solutions. As for consumers, they are harmed in both the short and long term. In the short term, they must pay a substantial extra cost to access a technology covered by a multiplicity of patents. In the future, they risk being deprived of new goods if the next generation of innovators move away from innovation.

To ensure a stable and sustainable balance in the system, legislators and judicial institutions in different countries should consider ways to limit patent inflation. This could be done by encouraging applicants and holders of patent portfolios to favor quality over quantity.

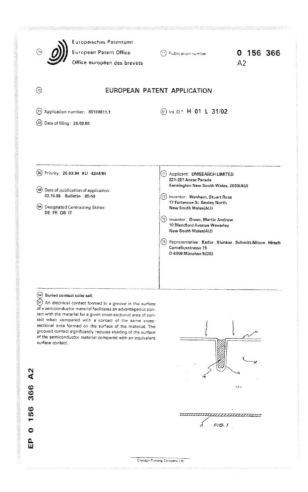

European patent application filed in 1985
by Martin Green and Stuart Wenham
on a buried contact solar cell.

For this invention which increases the energy conversion efficiency of solar cells,
Green et Wenham et received the European Inventor Award
from the European Patent Office in 2006.

Environmental challenges

The patent and sustainable development

The large numbers of patent filings mentioned in the previous chapter masks another reality: the increase in the scope of industrial production and consumption worldwide. Nowadays, there are countless companies of all sizes that want to bring new products and services to the market in an endless race for growth. Competing offers of equivalent or similar products and services are legion. This abundance of offers is mirrored by limitless consumption on the part of users who are always in a hurry to get the latest products. While this cycle undeniably benefits the economy, it is not without environmental consequences and contributes to resource depletion, pollution and climate change. The alarm signals that nature sends us are a warning about the way we interact with it. To ensure the sustainability of our kind and our environment, we have a collective responsibility to direct our actions with a long-term view in mind.

Patents are not responsible for the overproduction or overconsumption of goods, but they can be one indicator, among others, of these phenomena, as well as of efforts to contain them and protect the environment. For example, the Organization for Economic Co-operation and Development (OECD) uses patent information to measure global innovation in environment-related technologies. Similarly, in 2017, the European Patent Office (EPO) cooperated with the International Renewable Energy Agency (IRENA) to provide data on the latest trends in innovation and dissemination of climate change mitigation technologies. The findings of this cooperation contain reasons for hope: the number of inventions related to climate change technologies, especially in the field of renewable energy, is increasing worldwide.

Moreover, as we have seen previously, patents have the capacity to orient technical change by making technical sectors that are not naturally attractive appear so to inventors. This characteristic can be a major asset if it is put to the service of sustainable development projects. Timid attempts in this direction have already been made. For example, in 2009, the United Kingdom, followed by several other countries, set up a program to accelerate the examination of patent applications for green innovations. With this program, "green" patents can be issued in just a few months, compared to the delay of several years faced in other technical fields. This time saving benefits applicants by theoretically enabling them to attract investors or grant licenses earlier on. However, the acceleration of the procedure also has some disadvantages, such as forcing applicants to incur important costs sooner. Similarly, with the aim to encourage contributions that might lay the foundations for a sustainable future, the EPO regularly grants its European Inventor Award to rewards inventors of innovative technical solutions in the fields of renewable energy, "green" batteries, fuel cells, biomass and water consumption, among others. Highlighting these virtuous solutions sends a positive message to the public and may inspire young engineers to pursue a meaningful and useful topic of research.

However, these initiatives are still limited in number and scope. Additional patent-related incentives could be imagined in order to further guide innovation towards nature-friendly solutions. These could include reductions in official fees, facilities for licensing and specific labels for patents on green technologies. Patents alone are not capable of radically changing habits, but they undoubtedly have an interesting contribution to make as part of a global incentive policy designed to commit companies and society more strongly to the aims of sustainable development.

CONCLUSION

Here we are at the end of our exploration, which began in 14th century Venice. As a conclusion, let us ask ourselves this question: does the history of the patent contain lessons that allow us to predict its future? It is impossible, of course, to foresee what tomorrow will bring. However, two main constants emerge from our analysis of the past that may well continue to accompany the patent into the future.

The first constant is the surprising capacity of the patent to transform itself to fit the ideas of its time. Whether used to emancipate inventors from the severity of the Italian guilds, escape the arbitrariness and abuses of royal privileges in England, recognize a property right over inventions compatible with the ideas of the French Revolution, promote technical progress in the newly formed United States, or move between protectionism, universalism and cooperation between peoples, the patent has found a new justification at each period of history. While the main principles of the patent (i.e. granting temporary exclusivity to inventors in exchange for a benefit to society) have remained largely unchanged, its parameters (i.e. specifications, claims, terms, costs, scope, etc.) have continuously changed until taking the quasi-standardized TRIPS Agreement form that we know today. The patent's remarkable plasticity is certainly what has enabled it to survive the many political and economic upheavals that the world has experienced over the last six centuries. It is also, in part, what explains the spread of the patent across almost the entire planet and, with the exception of the short Dutch chapter at the end of the 19th century, the fact that it has never been discontinued. Despite their diversity, each society finds its own interest in keeping this instrument in place.

The second constant observed is the critical attention that the patent has received. It would be wrong to believe that the adoption of a patent system by almost every country in the world indicates total support on the part of the people. The temptation of those like the old guilds to entirely rely on the alternative protection of secrecy; the doubts expressed very early on by some of the founding fathers of the American nation; the frustrations felt by British users like Charles Dickens' hero Old John towards the patent during the Victorian era; the open hostility to the patent caused by the wave of economic liberalism in 19th century Europe; or the recent accusations of patent-based neo-colonialism launched against developed countries are only a few examples of the distrust that the patent has faced up to now. The current debate around the patent "waiver" in the context of the Covid-19 pandemic vividly illustrates the divisions that still exist around this tool today. Doubts and discords about patents will undoubtedly arise in the future as well, and will certainly take new forms.

Will one of these two opposing forces – support to or distrust of the patent – definitively prevail over the other in the future? There is no way of knowing for sure, and it is possible that they will continue to coexist, in permanent tension, for many centuries to come. However, the huge challenges ahead could change this situation. The highly sophisticated technologies of the fourth Industrial Revolution, as well as health and environmental risks, are likely to generate significant frictions within the current patent system. Moreover, our modern societies face several trends whereby traditions inherited from the past are challenged. There is no guarantee that future generations will not want to move away from patents if they perceive them as incompatible with their new ways of thinking. Finally, other problems stem from the patent system itself: one may wonder whether the exponential inflation of the number of patents is not the danger most likely to make the system a victim of its own success. To overcome these challenges, the patent system will therefore have to make use, more than ever before, of its extraordinary capacity to adapt.

In the end, as an instrument for protecting inventions, is not the patent itself an expression of human genius? It is only for the future to judge.

POSTFACE

In the first part of this book, Pascal Attali takes the reader on a fascinating journey through the history of patents – from the arsenal of Venice to negotiations at the World Trade Organization – thus putting into perspective the construction of a major institution of contemporary societies. He also provides the keys to better understand, in the second part of the book, the extent of the challenges associated with patents in the 21st century.

What are the moral and economic justifications for patent law? How has its use evolved in the era of the knowledge economy? How does the patent system adapt to the challenges of globalisation, digital technology and sustainable development? The care taken by Pascal Attali to document these questions and to develop his arguments on a broad range of themes such as artificial intelligence, the mitigation of climate change, or the fight against pandemics is commendable. This makes his book an important reference at a time when innovation is set to play an ever more central role in society and the economy.

Once upon a time, the patent offers the reader a clear and scholarly overview of the world of patents. As such, it will arouse the interest of both industrial property specialists and laypersons wishing to better understand patents and the debates they may arouse.

Yann Ménière[1]
Chief economist of the European Patent Office

---

[1] The views and opinions expressed in this afterword are those of Yann Ménière and do not necessarily reflect the official policy or position of the European Patent Office.

ACKNOWLEDGEMENTS

This book would not be what it is without the careful proofreading and advice of Sophie Enos-Attali. I would like to thank her warmly here.

I would also like to express my deep gratitude to Pascal Faure, Director General of the French National Institute of Industrial Property (INPI) and to Yann Ménière, Chief Economist of the European Patent Office (EPO), for their trust and interest in my work.

Finally, I would like to thank Aude Marty, François-Xavier de Beaufort, Valérie Hochet and Bérangère Deleau for their kind support.

BIBLIOGRAPHY

ABRAMOWICZ M., 2003. Perfecting Patent Prizes. In : *Vanderbilt Law Review*. Vol. 56, Issue 1, Article 3, pp. 115-236.

ADAMS J., 2019. History of the patent system. In : Takenaka, Toshiko (ed), *Research Handbook on Patent Law and Theory*, Edward Elgar Publishing. Chapter 1.

ANDERSON G and TOLLISON R., 1993. Barristers and Barriers : Sir Edward Coke and the Regulation of Trade. In : *Cato Journal*. Vol.13, N°1.

BEAUCHAMP C., 2016. The First Patent Litigation Explosion. In : *The Yale Law Journal*. Vol. 125, N°4, pp. 848-944.

BELFANTI, C. (2006). Between mercantilism and market: Privileges for invention in early modern Europe. In : *Journal of Institutional Economics, 2*(3), pp. 319-338.

BELTRAN A., CHAUVEAU S. and GALVEZ-BEHAR G., 2001. *Des brevets et des marques*. Paris : Fayard. ISBN 2-213-61011-8.

BERRY R., 2015. Researching the Early History of the Patent Policy: Getting Started. In : *Journal of the Patent & Trademark Resource,* Center Association 25.

INPI, 2001. *L'Institut national de la propriété industrielle : inventé pour les inventeurs*. Issy-les-Moulineaux : Creapress. ISBN 2-913449-02.

BOLDRIN M. and LEVINE D., 2013. The Case against Patents. In : *Journal of Economic Perspectives*. Vol. 27, N°1, Winter 2013, pp. 3-22.

BOGSCH A., 1992. *Les 25 premières années de l'Organisation Mondiale de la Propriété intellectuelle*. Genève : OMPI. ISBN 92-805-0431-2.

BURGER-HELMCHEN T., PENIN J., GUITTARD C., SCHENK E. and DINTRICH A., 2013. *L'innovation ouverte : Définition, pratiques et perspectives*. CCI Paris Ile-de-France. ISBN : 978-2-85504-591-7

CHESBROUGH H., 2003. *Open innovation: The new imperative for creating and profiting from technology*. USA : Harvard Business School Press. ISBN-10 : 1422102831 ; ISBN-13 : 978-1422102831.

CONDE C. and GUERRERO M., 2015. A Brief History of Patent Law: From Middle Age Privileges to WTO Rules. In : *Boletín Departamento Propiedad Intelectual*.

DICKENS C., 1850. *A Poor Man's Tale of a Patent*.

DIEBOLT C. and PELLIER K., 2009. Introduction: Vers une nouvelle histoire économique des brevets ? In : *Brussels Economic Review*, ULB - Universite Libre de Bruxelles. Vol. 52, N°3/4, pp. 204-214.

DIEBOLT C. and PELLIER K., 2009. Patents in the Long Run: Theory, History and Statistics. In : *History & Mathematics, 8. hal-02929514.*

GALVEZ-BEHAR G., 2009. L'État et les brevets d'invention (1791-1922) : une relation embarrassée. Colloque "Concurrence et marchés : droit et institutions du Moyen Âge à nos jours", Comité d'histoire économique et financière de la France, 10-11 décembre 2009. *Concurrence et marchés : droit et institutions du Moyen Âge à nos jours*, Dec 2009, Paris. ⟨halshs-00548184⟩

GALVEZ-BEHAR G., 2020. The 1883 Paris Convention and the Impossible Unification of Industrial Property, in Gooday, Graeme; Wilf, Steven (eds). *Patent Cultures: Diversity and Harmonization in Historical Perspective*, Cambridge University Press, pp.38-68.

GAUDILLIERE JP, 2008. How pharmaceuticals became patentable: the production and appropriation of drugs in the twentieth century. In : *History and Technology*. Vol. 24, N° 2, pp. 99-106

GRISET P. and LABORIE L., 2016. Entre mondialisation et intégration européenne : origines et signature de la Convention sur le brevet européen (Munich 1973). In : *Bulletin de l'Institut Pierre Renouvin*, 2016/2, N° 44, pp. 55-74.

KHAN B. Z., 2001. Innovations in Intellectual Property Systems and Economic Development. Yale University: New Haven.

KHAN B. Z., 2006. Economic History of Patents and Patent Institutions. In : *EH.Net Encyclopedia*, (ed) Robert Whaples.

KHAN B. Z., 2009. *The Democratization of Invention: Patents and Copyrights in American Economic Development, 1790-1920.* USA : NBER and Cambridge University Press. ISBN-13: 978-0521747202 ; ISBN-10: 0521747201.

KOSTYLO J., 2010. From Gunpowder to Print: The Common Origins of Copyright and Patent. In : Ronan Deazley, Martin Kretschmer and Lionel Bently (eds), *Privilege and Property: Essays on the History of Copyright*. Chapter 1, Cambridge, UK: Open Book Publishers, pp. 21-50.

KRANAKIS E., 2007. Patents and Power: European Patent-System Integration in the Context of Globalization. In : *Technology and Culture*, The Johns Hopkins University Press and the Society for the History of Technology. Vol. 48, N° 4, pp. 689-728.

LAPOINTE S., 2000. L'histoire des brevets. In : *Les Cahiers de la Propriété Intellectuelle*, Yvon Blais Inc. Vol. 12, N° 3.

LEMLEY M., 2016. The Surprising Resilience of the Patent System. In : *Texas Law Review*. Vol. 95:1, pp. 1-57.

LEVEQUE F. and MENIERE Y., 2004. The Economics of Patents and Copyright. Monograph. In : *Berkeley Electronic Press*. Available at SSRN: https://ssrn.com/abstract=642622

LONG P., 1991. Invention, Authorship, "Intellectual Property," and the Origin of Patents: Notes toward a Conceptual History. In : *Technology and Culture*. Vol. 32, No. 4, Special Issue: Patents and Invention (Oct.,1991), pp. 846-884.

MACHLUP F. and PENROSE E., 1950. The Patent Controversy in the Nineteenth Century. In : *The Journal of Economic History*. Vol. 10, N° 1, May 1950, pp. 1-29.

MADIGAN K. and MOSSOFF A., 2017. Turning Gold to Lead: How Patent Eligibility Doctrine Is Undermining U.S. Leadership in Innovation. In : *George Mason Law Review*. Vol. 24, pp. 939-960.

MALISSARD P., 2010. La propriété intellectuelle : origine et évolution. In : *Propriété intellectuelle et université : entre la libre circulation des idées et la privatisation des savoirs,* Chapitre 5. Québec : Presses de l'Université du Québec. ISBN : 2760525880.

MATHELY P., 1978. *Le Droit européen des brevets d'invention*. Paris : Librairie du Journal des notaires et des avocats. ISBN-10 : 2850280143 ; ISBN-13 : 978-2850280146.

MOSER P., 2005. How Do Patent Laws Influence Innovation? Evidence from Nineteenth-Century World Fairs. In : *American Economic Review*. 95, pp. 1214-1236.

MOSER P., 2013. Patents and Innovation: Evidence from Economic History. In : *Journal of Economic Perspectives*. Vol. 27, N° 1, pp. 23–44

MOSER P., 2016. Patents and Innovation in Economic History. In : *Annual Review of Economics*. Vol. 8(1), pp. 241-258.

MOSSOFF A., 2001. *Rethinking the Development of Patents: An Intellectual History, 1550-1800*, 52 Hastings L.J. 1255. Available at: https://repository.uchastings.edu/hastings_law_journal/vol52/iss6/2.

MOSSOFF A., 2007. Who Cares What Thomas Jefferson Thought about Patents - Reevaluating the Patent Privilege in Historical Context. In : Cornell Law Review. Vol. 92, pp. 953-1012.

MOSSOFF A., 2021. Pandemics, Patents, and Price Controls. In : *Legal Memorandum, Edwin Meese III Center for Legal & Judicial Studies, The Heritage Foundation*. May 13, 2021. N°285.

MOSSOFF A., 2021. The Covid-19 Intellectual Property Waiver: Threats to U.S. Innovation, Economic Growth, and National Security. In : *Legal Memorandum, Edwin Meese III Center for Legal & Judicial Studies, The Heritage Foundation*. September 17, 2021. N°290.

NASCIMENTO M., 2016. The First Patents and the Rise of Glass Technology. In : *Recent Innovations in Chemical Engineering*. Vol. 9, N° 1, pp. 20-30.

OEB/EPO, 1983. Convention sur le brevet européen : La conférence diplomatique de Munich, 10 ans après. In : *Journal officiel de l'Office européen des brevets.* 21 septembre 1983, 6ᵉ année / N° 9, pp. 361-406.

OEB/EPO, 2021. *Patent Index 2020 : Statistics at a glance.*

OMPI, 2021. *WIPO IP Facts and Figures 2020.* Genève : WIPO Publication No. 943E/20. ISBN 978-92-805-3208-1.

PENIN J. and NEICU D., 2018. Patents and Open Innovation: Bad Fences Do Not Make Good Neighbors. In : *Journal of Innovation Economics & Management.* 2018/1, N° 25, pp. 57-85.

PENIN J., 2010. Le problème des "patent trolls" : comment limiter la spéculation sur la propriété intellectuelle dans une économie fondée sur les connaissances ? In : *Innovations.* 2010/2, N° 32, pp. 35-53.

PLASSERAUD Y. and SAVIGNON F., 1983. *Paris 1883. Genèse du droit unioniste des brevets.* Paris : Litec. ISBN 2-71-110455-9.

PLASSERAUD Y. and SAVIGNON F., 1986. *L'Etat et l'invention : Histoire des brevets.* Paris : La Documentation Française. ISBN 2-11-001647-7.

ROSEN W., 2010. *The Most Powerful Idea in the World: A Story of Steam, Industry, and Invention.* USA : The University Chicago Press. ISBN-13: 978-0-226-72634-2 ; ISBN-10: 0-226-72634-7.

SICHELMAN T. and O'CONNOR S., 2012. Patents as Promoters of Competition: The Guild Origins of Patent Law in the Venetian Republic. In : San Diego Law Review. Vol. 49: 1267.

STIGLITZ J., 2007. Prizes, Not Patents. In : *Project Syndicate.* 6 Mars 2007. Disponible à https://www.project-syndicate.org/commentary/prizes--not-patents?barrier=accesspaylog

USPTO, 2021. *Trademarks and patents in China: The impact of non-market factors on filing trends and IP systems.*

VAN GOMPEL S., 2019. Patent Abolition: A Real-Life Historical Case Study. In *: American University International Law Review.* Vol. 34, Issue 4, Article 6.

WRIGHT B., 1983. The Economics of Invention Incentives: Patents, Prizes, and Research Contracts. In : *The American Economic Review.* Vol. 73, N° 4, pp. 691-707.

TABLE OF CONTENTS

Printed in Great Britain
by Amazon

44169975R00169